Danesholme

C000180114

CD	✓✓		
4/08	2/10		

Please return/renew this item by the last date shown. Books may also be renewed by 'phone and the Internet

Northamptonshire Libraries and Information Service

 **Northamptonshire County Council**

www.northamptonshire.gov.uk/leisure/libraries/

Paul Fox © Copyright 2006

All rights reserved

British Library Cataloguing In Publication Data
A Record of this Publication is available
from the British Library

ISBN 1846850835
978-1-84685-083-7

First Published 2006 by

Exposure Publishing, an imprint of Diggory Press,
Three Rivers, Minions, Liskeard, Cornwall, PL14 5LE, UK
WWW.DIGGORYPRESS.COM

For Rachael

CHAPTER ONE
When Did It All Begin?

I OPENED my eyes. Suddenly, it was pitch black. All I could see were the luminous hands of my watch. It was ten past three in the morning. I leaned over and switched on the bedside lamp; as my eyes adjusted to the light, I sat on the edge of the bed and looked around the room. It was just like any of the 100 hotel rooms that I had stayed in: the comfortable bed, small television set and en suite bathroom in one corner. This, however, was not a hotel room. I closed my eyes and shuddered when I realised that I was far from being in a comfortable hotel room looking forward to a day of appointments with clients or staff from a regional office.

This was a room in a psychiatric wing of a private hospital.

So I knew where I was, and why the room seemed so familiar to me. It was more than that. I couldn't work it out at first but then it came to me. The reason why this room looked so familiar was because it was almost identical to the one that I'd stayed in on my Initial Officers' Training Course at Royal Air Force Cranwell. How could it be? What sort of a building firm would specialise in military establishments and psychiatric hospitals? But there it was — the room was identical, their layout was identical and yet the situation in which I found myself couldn't be more different.

At RAF Cranwell my room was full of the paraphernalia of military life. Highly polished shoes and various uniforms hung around the room, the order of the day pinned to the notice board. The door propped open so that anyone could call in with a funny story or a problem to be shared. How we laughed. How hard we worked that week to pass the final exams on Friday, and as Course Leader, how pleased and proud I was that not only had I passed the Course but so had everyone else.

The room I was now in was full of the paraphernalia of hospital life. A few charts on the wall with my name on them. The door propped open — not by choice this time — but so I could be observed every 15 minutes by a member of the nursing staff. I got up and walked round the bed; a brown folder lay next to yesterday's unread newspaper. I picked it up, opened it and recognized that it must have been left by the previous occupant of my room. In bold letters the inside sheet read as follows:

- severe clinical depression
- alcohol dependent?
- anorexic/ bulimic
- self-harm (feet?)

Then the full horror of my situation struck me like somebody hitting me in the face. The file had my name on it, my date of birth, my full address, and my doctor's name. I closed my eyes and sank back down. Suddenly a huge coloured guy was standing over me.

'Are you OK, Paul?' he asked in a deep South African accent. 'Can I get you anything?'

'No, thanks,' I replied. I felt so embarrassed. I just wanted him to go. He seemed to sense this and stood very close to me and said, 'You know, Paul, this is a really good place. The doctors here can really help you.'

I didn't answer but he tried again and said, 'How long have you been ill for?' I knew I wasn't gonna get away with not speaking, so after a long pause, I said, 'Quite some time.' After an even longer pause, he said, 'I know it's difficult for you but try to think back to before you became ill. Try to remember the good times in your life and perhaps try and think back to when all this started.'

Realising that conversation was going to be very difficult, he turned and as he got to the door he said, 'I'm just at the end of the corridor if you need anything.' I didn't say anything. I just nodded.

His words seemed to echo round the room and realising that it was going to be impossible for me to sleep that night, I decided to devote what little control I had of my mind to try to find out when it had all started.

If instead of reading this you were watching a film or video of my story, this is where the screen would go shaky and my voice would start softly and then boom out of the speakers, repeating itself over and over, 'When did it all start?' 'When did it all start?' 'When did it all start?'

As I lay on the bed and closed my eyes, my mind went back almost ten years to the day. I was coming in the front door for the second time that morning, having started the car on the drive, and I was beginning to gather my things together for the start of the working day. It was 8 o'clock in the morning. Catherine, my wife, was still in her dressing-gown and tried to talk to me as I gathered the newspaper, my briefcase, my overcoat and roughly tucked them under my arm. We were going on holiday the next day and Catherine was asking me to get home early so I could help with the packing.

'Yes, yes, of course I'll be home early,' I said, trying to reassure her. 'You know how I hate packing and I am still not sure about Daniel's cough.' I held her arms and said, 'Look, I'll be home early and Daniel will be fine. This will be the best holiday ever.'

She gave me a look as if to say you're going to be home late and Daniel's cough is something that I will have to deal with, but before she could answer I'd made a run for the car and roared off down the road at full speed for the office.

Catherine, naturally, was right. Indeed I did try to get home early that night but with this and that, it was nearly 7 o'clock before I put my key in the door. I quickly found the children in the living room watching a video. They didn't seem as buoyant as I was expecting and Daniel's face was still very red. After whipping them up into a frenzy of excitement about tomorrow's big adventure I determined that I would have been better off leaving them to the video, so I set off to find Catherine upstairs in our bedroom.

Catherine was packing two large suitcases. She didn't acknowledge me and thankfully, didn't mention the time of my arrival, despite my promises that morning, but as if on autopilot started asking questions about how many pairs of shorts did she think I needed and what aftershave I would like to take on holiday.

'Just my white shorts please and I think I will take the Christian Dior aftershave — the one you like.' Catherine didn't answer but quickly found the shorts and the aftershave. 'And your blue sweatshirt?'

'Yes, yes, that'll be fine.' I answered, hoping soon to be able to switch the conversation to what a wonderful holiday we were going to have in Florida. By now the children had joined us in the bedroom and as fast as Catherine was packing suitcases they were unpacking or trying to talk to Catherine at the same time. I, naturally, didn't help at all, but went into the bathroom and started to take my suit off.

All of a sudden it seemed to be very quiet and very still. I couldn't hear the children's voices in the room next to me. There seemed to be a low rumbling sound like an approaching earthquake, then a huge eruption of noise. I instinctively knew what it was. It was Catherine's eve of holiday speech, and delivered at full volume beginning with the words, 'I'm never going on holiday again.'

Opening the bathroom door in my underpants, I stepped into the bedroom looking for some clothes that hadn't been packed to wear. I listened to the quieter second half of her speech, including the now familiar bit about 'Why don't you take the children on holiday on your own? I'd just be grateful for a rest for two weeks.'

I nodded a few times said, 'OK' a few times, and then headed for the kitchen to make some tea: Catherine's antidote!

After a cup of tea Catherine had calmed down enough to finish packing. Feeling guilty that I had done nothing at all to help, I decided to find the children and see if I could encourage them to have an early night. To my surprise they were already in bed asleep. 'Strange,' I thought. 'I never used to sleep at all before I went on holiday and we only went to places like Great Yarmouth or if really lucky a holiday camp somewhere, let alone a two-week extravaganza in America's playgrounds, including three days in Disney World and a trip to the John F. Kennedy Space Centre.'

That night we didn't get much sleep. The children didn't wake through excitement, but Daniel's cough was really beginning to get a hold, and because Catherine and I were both very concerned about Daniel, we didn't seem to notice that Victoria was also awake and looking very pale. Well, I am sure that Catherine noticed but I didn't. I could only think of the coming two weeks.

As we set out for the airport the next morning the signs were not good; the children were quiet and very pale and now they were both coughing.

We got through the formalities of checking in and as we made our way to the aircraft I finally thought, 'Well, this is it. We are off on our holiday of a lifetime.' The first sign of trouble came as soon as the aircraft was airborne and Daniel was promptly sick — you are probably thinking it went everywhere but it didn't. Thanks to Catherine's lightning reaction and amazing perception, she managed to analyse and execute the manoeuvre of opening the sick bag and with a nanosecond left before we were all covered in diced carrots (why is it always diced carrots when children are sick?) was able to negotiate with Daniel to use the bag. Three seconds later you would have thought nothing was wrong. There was only a slightly watery-eyed Daniel, and Catherine was holding an expertly folded sick bag for the Flight Attendant to take away. 'Do you think he will be OK now?' I asked Catherine. 'I think so,' she said, reassuring me but not herself.

By the time we landed at Orlando things were far from okay with both children. We had managed to go through the card in terms of using all the sick bags, being moved to the back of the aircraft for the majority of the flight, speaking to all the flight attendants, and dragging an unsuspecting passenger, who just happened to be a doctor, out of first class, who was helpful and sympathetic and reassured us that there was nothing seriously wrong but it would be advisable to get them checked out as soon as we landed. For the last hour of the journey we were moved to first class so that we could get off the aircraft quickly in order to get the children to the hotel or remain on board for medical assistance. None of the extravagance managed to lighten my mood. By this time Catherine was near hysteria but only I knew; to everyone else she appeared calm, fragrant and in control. Only I recognised the mad staring eyes and the speed at which she confirmed she was fine. To the question 'How are you?' Catherine's reply of 'fine' came back at me like a bullet.

We declined the offer of medical assistance and sprinted from the aircraft dragging both children as quickly as we could to immigration. Unbelievably, we were the first there and cleared immigration within ten minutes. Whilst waiting for our bags both the children seemed to cheer up when they saw a lady approaching us with a dog. Not normally a family of dog-lovers I was pleased that at least they were taking an interest in their surroundings and amazingly both reaching out to stroke the dog. As Catherine and I looked at one another, smiled and both said 'Aarh' together, I failed to notice that this dog had a handler, a thirty-something female wearing an over vest with an official warning on it — it read something like 'Official U.S. Agency for Foodstuffs arriving illegally. Do not attempt to apprehend this Marshall from the course of official business. For more information speak to your lawyer, your social worker or visit our web site www.dontfuckusabout.com.'

Anyway it said something like that and just as I was about to go into my 'I'm with the Koreans on dogs' routine, I realised that the woman was talking. 'Can I ask you a few questions, Sir?' Before I could reply she launched straight into her no doubt well-rehearsed routine. 'Are you the head of this family?'

'Yes,' I replied, trying to look serious and co-operative and realising that the dog was about to savage me at any second — well would have savaged me at any second as soon as it had finished the plastic Power Ranger that Daniel was feeding it.

Another question hit me: 'Which country have you arrived from?' I was going to reply 'England' along with my speech about 'shame we knocked down Hadrian's Wall.' Along with 'Welshmen are only Irishmen who can swim.' But one look at Catherine's now foot wide eyes warned me that this was not the time or place.

'United Kingdom,' I replied.

'Are you carrying any foodstuffs, breads, milk?'

'Is that all?' I thought. Surely this dog toting neo-Nazi was going to ask me something more relevant like whether I had brought a ham sandwich into the U.S.

I waited for her to finish but she already had and was now looking at me as if I were something stuck to the bottom of her shoe. When she said foodstuffs, I was thinking of the weekly shop at Asda: half a car full of Catherine's expertly planned shopping, covering everything from every type of food, drink and cleaning product available to man, not a half eaten bar of chocolate and a couple of uneaten oranges that had survived somehow the children's welcome packs from Virgin Airlines, but I didn't know that then.

'Are you sure?' she fixed me with a steely grin. Even the dog looked up. I managed to gather myself and answered her clearly, straightforwardly, in my best B.B.C. Essex voice.

'No, we do not have any foodstuffs at all'. At that moment our bags arrived on the carousel. The dog started to take a lot more interest. Suddenly she let the dog off the lead and instead of leaping for my throat, as I thought it would do, it dived onto the children's rucksacks, tail wagging like mad. I was surprised that a small crowd had not gathered.

We were obviously drug runners about to be busted and how awful that they had used the children's rucksacks to conceal their deadly cargo. But no, everyone else was carrying on as normal. The dog's tail was wagging so hard that it was beginning to rock from side to side, and just as I was beginning to wonder where this was all going to end, she said, 'What about the oranges the children got on the flight? Are they in their rucksacks?'

Stunned with the trivial line of questioning and knowing if I said anything I would definitely end up in a U.S. jail and Catherine definitely wouldn't come and get me out, Catherine took over the answering of the questions.

'Yes, they did get oranges and yes, they are in their rucksacks. Would you like them?' Catherine said as charmingly as possible. The Nazi and the dog took notice of what Catherine said. The oranges were quickly retrieved. The dog and the Nazi were happy as they were handed over and she left as quickly as she has arrived.

'Silly cow,' I said to Catherine.

With that brush with officialdom out of the way, the children looking and sounding better, we headed for the car rental desk. As we were on a package deal the holiday came with a rental car. A car we could all get in and would meet our needs perfectly. A car suitable for two adults, one 4-year-old and one 9-year-old. That was Catherine's understanding. To my mind, this was going to be the holiday of a lifetime and the car that came with the holiday was not going to be suitable for me.

As we made our way up the queue, Catherine expertly read my mind.

'You're not going to upgrade the car, are you?' she asked.

As Catherine is able to read my mind, she didn't need to ask the question, as she knew that answer already — of course I was going to upgrade the car. This was America, the mothership to all petrol heads and if there is anything I do like on this earth, it is cars - ask anyone. And particularly at that time, it was American cars. Driving along the freeway in the U.S. to me...well, it is like automotive pornography!

As I am sure you will have by now realised, my expectations of this holiday were not only high. They were sky high. We had had our setbacks on the way. It had been a very strenuous year at work. We had planned this holiday and I was not going to be happy with anything second rate. By the time I got to the front desk I was like a kid in a sweetshop.

After handing over our documents, the clerk tapped in a few details to the computer and said, 'Mr. Fox, we have a car for you but would you like to upgrade?'

Before the last word had left his mouth, 'Yes,' I said.

'Oh, O.K'.

'What do you fancy?' recognising that this was his lucky day.

'What have you got?' I said.

To Catherine this was just a delaying tactic. Other people at other desks already had their car keys and were waiting by a small concrete island where perfectly good looking, shiny, clean, cars were being delivered to them. I, on the other hand, was oblivious to all this. The children were looking tired and hot, yet I was going through the entire inventory of Budget Rent a Car to see if anything would be suitable.

Finally the clerk said, 'What about a Lincoln?'

'Town Car?' I said.

'Yep,' came the reply.

'Latest model?'

'You got it'.

'Power everything?'

'That's the one'.

Then the clincher. 'It's white, red leather interior and has only got 14 miles on the clock'.

'I'll take it'.

Catherine, I could see, was pleased. Well, if she wasn't pleased, she was just glad to make it to the concrete island and on our way to the hotel. After paying the guy one arm and one leg, signing and initialling 50 forms, and promising the guy one of my kidneys if I crashed it, we set off for the concrete island. It was worth the wait. Five minutes later a beautiful white Lincoln turned the corner and headed for us. Everybody in the queue gasped and pointed. Well, no, actually only the men. Well, most of the men. The rest of them were thinking 'Christ, it's the drug dealers and they have even had the cheek to rent a drug dealer's car.'

The Lincoln was fantastic. The children were impressed with the rear seats that reclined like the ones in the front. Catherine also seemed to be impressed, probably because we were at long last on our way to the hotel and she was sitting at least six feet away from me on the front bench seat. As we pulled out of the rental compound I glanced over at Catherine, peered at the children on the back seat and said 'We are on our way. This is going to be the holiday of a lifetime'. I pulled onto the freeway and set off in search of our hotel in completely the wrong direction!

After an interesting look at downtown Orlando's industrial centre we found our hotel after taking a few minutes to row with the security guard on the gate. Asking the manager of the hotel to help me open the boot of our hire car, we made it at last to our room.

Within just a few minutes the suitcases were open, and naturally, Catherine's expert packing meant that all our nightclothes were easy to handle and hardly creased at all from the long flight. The children fell instantly to sleep. As we got into bed I said to Catherine 'I'm sure that they will be OK in the morning. The sun will be shining and we can start our holiday'.

Early the next morning I got up and looked out the window. The sun wasn't shining; it wasn't exactly overcast but it was far from the golden sunshine I had hoped to see. Daniel was next up and he seemed to have shrugged off the symptoms of the previous day. Victoria, however, was not at all well.

The next three days were spent in our hotel room. Daniel had improved enough for me to take him on short trips along International Drive, stopping for fast food and looking around some of the small shopping malls. You have to understand at this point that although Daniel and Victoria had little more than a touch of flu the effect it was having on me was far out of proportion to their symptoms.

My wonderful holiday of a lifetime was turning into a disaster. Of course I thought only of myself. Catherine had not moved from the hotel room at all during the three days. It didn't seem to get her down. She just accepted that there was very little that we could do until both children were fully functioning. While Victoria slept, Catherine spent her time reading up about the local area and working out a revised holiday itinerary.

By day four, however, the situation was a lot better. After sleeping for virtually three days Victoria felt well enough to go out. The sun started to shine and so we decided to head off for a quiet day at Sea World, Catherine pointing out quite rightly that this was the closest attraction and if the children did feel unwell we could go back to the hotel quickly.

As soon as we arrived in Sea World, we had our photograph taken, and looking at the photograph now, it speaks volumes. Catherine looks serene, and the children look happy to be there, if a little fragile. I look like someone who is about to go into battle: gritted teeth, locked limbs, a look of someone who is far from relaxed and really I don't belong in the photo.

As we swept through Sea World I felt something well up inside me. I couldn't work out how many days we had wasted. Why did it matter? We had only lost a couple of days; the children hadn't intentionally become ill. Why did it all matter so much?

Looking back now from my room at The Priory, perhaps that was when it started, this sort of overwhelming anxiety for no real reason. After all, we were on holiday. Why couldn't I just get on and enjoy it like everybody else?

As it was approaching lunchtime, Catherine suggested we started looking for somewhere to eat. You're never very far from somewhere to eat, so we soon found ourselves in a very large McDonald's type restaurant. Catherine and the children found a table and I went off to get the food.

Little did I know that what happened next would have a long lasting and profound effect on my life and would lead me ultimately to The Priory.

About halfway through my meal of chicken sandwich and fries I was aware I had a pain. Catherine can read my mind, as I have already told you, so as soon as I knew, Catherine knew. Catherine's eyes fixed on me and she said, 'Have you got a pain?'

'No, of course, I haven't,' I replied. I could see Catherine wasn't convinced so I took a large gulp of Coca-Cola just to prove I was all right. I was then acutely aware that the pain had got much worse. It seemed to be spreading from the central part of my throat down into my chest. The Coca-Cola had gone down and was coming back up into my mouth. Recognizing that something was wrong, Catherine said, 'Do you need to get at some fresh air?'

I just nodded, got up from my seat and walked a short distance to the door. By now I had got used to the air-conditioned interior of the restaurant and so the heat outside hit me and seemed to increase the pain in my throat. I spat the Coca-Cola out into a nearby plant. As I looked up I saw that I had caught the attention of an American family sitting on a bench. The mum, dad and two kids — a boy and girl just like my own family. What was different was their size. I just could not believe how fat they all were.

Before I left the office one of my colleagues told me that Disneyland was the fat capital of the world. Looking at this family I could believe it. They were all dressed in Lycra shorts and matching shirts and it seemed to me that they were gorging themselves on huge burgers, overflowing with cheese and bacon, and resting in what looked like a small bucket was a mountain of french fries. All of them looked at me as they gulped down their diet Coke. The irony was not lost on me: as if diet Coke was going to make a scrap of difference to the calorie content of their meal.

But I wasn't laughing. The pain in my chest now seemed to be restricting my movement and I was taking shallower and shallower breaths and the pain was increasing. I was aware that Catherine was looking at me, and amazingly, as I am not a brave person and determined that nothing else was going to delay our holiday, I walked back into the restaurant and sat down as if nothing were wrong.

Catherine wasn't quite as good at reading my mind this time. 'Do you feel better now?' she said.

I just nodded and reached for a french fry; this was a huge mistake as I couldn't swallow the french fry. It wouldn't go down and when it came back up into my mouth my chest felt as though it was gripped in a vice set on fire. I was beginning to fight for air and then began to choke. Catherine was on her feet and round to me.

Instantly the children stopped eating and looked at me worriedly. The room started to spin. I got up quickly and knocked my chair over backwards. Everybody looked round. Catherine was trying to calm me and the children, and was looking round for someone to help her. I thought I was dying. I couldn't get air inside my lungs and my throat was blocked.

A lady from a nearby table came over to me. She told Catherine that she was a nurse. I couldn't speak but I remember her taking my pulse. Just before I lost consciousness I saw Victoria running for help and I remember seeing the faces of what seemed like thousands of people looking at me. After that it's all a bit of a blur. Apparently the emergency services arrived very quickly and I regained consciousness just as an oxygen mask was being placed on my face.

At the Emergency Medical Centre I was examined by a doctor and quickly given the all clear. I remember the doctor asking me what was the last thing I had tried to eat and I told him it was a french fry. He looked at Catherine and I knowingly and said 'Aargh' rather reassuringly, and went on to explain that french fries in the USA sometimes have a coating on them to make them shiny. For some reason some British visitors found them difficult to swallow. He then went on to discuss allergic reactions and suggested that I talk to my G.P. about this on my return home.

However, I did not explain that I had had the pain long before the french fry. I was just pleased to get on with our dream holiday.

I walked out of the consulting room and confirmed to Catherine and the children that I was perfectly all right and I wanted to resume our tour. I could see that Catherine had her doubts but she went along with me this time. The children, however, were not so forgiving and for the first time I saw that they did not believe what I was saying, but knew better than to mention it. I should have understood then that everything had now changed.

This was not the first time I had had a pain in my throat and I knew that I was going to have to do something about it when I returned. Something else happened as well: the overwhelming anxiety with all of the symptoms of dizziness, shortness of breath, etc., were still with me. In fact from that moment on, it was with me more or less all of the time.

What I hadn't understood was the profound effect my performance had had on the children and Catherine. Whenever we ate a meal together, the children would look at me for signs of choking. If I took Daniel out on his own we could just not call into McDonald's or Burger King like we used to. He was worried that I would choke. So it was easier for me not to eat in front of the children, thinking I was doing the right thing. But it wasn't. The anxiety over eating lasted not only the rest of the holiday but it is still with me today.

*****

As I looked around the walls of my room I decided I should now try and sleep. It was now coming up for 5 o'clock in the morning. I was still being checked by the South African nurse every 15 minutes. Just as I reached for the light switch I saw him again in the doorway.

'You still awake, Paul?' he said. I just nodded. 'Seeing as you are awake, I forgot to ask you what you would like for breakfast.'

'Nothing,' I said as I pulled the duvet over my head.

'Paul, you have got to have something,' he said.

'Wanna bet?'

Click went the light switch and I was in darkness again.

CHAPTER TWO
First Days

AS I had stayed awake for most of the night you would have thought that I would be anxious to sleep in later in the morning, but I was wide awake by 7.30. Unlike RAF Cranwell there was very little noise. I didn't really know what to expect, as I had never been in a psychiatric hospital before.

But in actual fact this wasn't exactly true. I had been to this one before, to visit a client. It was five years ago and the client had won the National Lottery and he had a substantial sum invested via my company. His financial adviser was Keith in my office. Not only a colleague but a very good friend, Keith was on holiday and so his post came to me. There was an urgent declaration for this particular client to sign from an investment company.

Realising its importance I asked my secretary, Sue, to arrange an appointment for later in the week. Sue had arranged the appointment with the client at somewhere called The Priory and later when I was discussing work appointments with her she explained that he'd been taken into hospital and it was OK to go and see him there. A couple of days later I found myself in their car park and I went into reception and was escorted to his room.

I ascertained at this point, with some horror, that his room was next door to where I now found myself. I remembered the meeting well.

Jim was a man in his late fifties. He didn't move from the bed as I walked into his room. I tried to engage in small talk, but he didn't seem interested, so I turned instead to the papers that I had brought with me. Without a word he took my pen and signed the forms where Sue had helpfully made a small cross. As soon as this was done, he seemed to want me to go, so I wished him well and got up to leave.

For some reason he decided to walk with me to the door of the ward. On the way I explained that I would deal with the paperwork, and that Keith would be back in a fortnight's time and would be in touch with Jim as soon as he got into the office. Even though I knew nothing of his condition I said, 'I'm sure you'll be at home by then'.

'I don't know,' he said. 'Just depends on how I'm feeling and if the depression has lifted by then.'

This didn't exactly open the floodgates of conversation but we did stand and talk for a while about our shared interest of the Air Training Corps. Jim had been instrumental in me reviving my interest in the A.T.C. and I was now heavily involved (more of that later). He asked after my Dad, as they shared the same Royal Marines heritage and when I left him he was smiling and seemed to be in a much better mood.

But as I walked out to the car I could not help thinking about what he had said. Depression. He was in hospital because of depression. I asked myself, 'Surely there has got to be more to it than that?' Perhaps he has had some operation as well and perhaps he was just recuperating there, perhaps feeling a bit low. Sometimes general anaesthetic can affect you like that.

In truth anything affects me — just ask Catherine. After one Paracetamol I seem to slow down and if I have to take two, I normally sleep for a day. I was unfortunate enough to have to have some major dental surgery about ten years ago and the hospital gave me Pethidine. When they gave me the tablets at the hospital just before I was driven home, Catherine suggested very strongly that I not take them until I got indoors. 'What do you know?' I mumbled. Catherine gave me a resigned look as I swilled down the tablets.

What I had forgotten was that Catherine had given birth to our son three months earlier and if you think my knowledge of mental illness at that time was pretty scant, I can assure you I knew even less about childbirth. Having spent most of the time Catherine was in labour at the office or with clients (please don't write) Pethidine is something that Catherine and most mums know all about.

By the time we had driven the 20 minutes back to our house not only couldn't I speak but also I couldn't feel the lower half of my body. A neighbour had to be summoned to help Catherine carry me into the house and up to bed. I then slept for three days.

As you will read later 'everything to excess' is almost my middle name, but the only thing I haven't done is take any form of recreational drug. I honestly think whatever I took would have had such a bad effect on me that it would probably have made News at Ten. The headline would have been something like 'Financial Adviser comatose for three months — clients haven't noticed.' Or what's the other one? The one that speeds you up? If I took that I would be high as a kite literally and no doubt would be found clinging to someone's ceiling or running the marathon while dictating a book all at the same time. So tablets and I just don't mix.

'Depression', I thought, 'how can he be depressed about anything?' I had just looked at the credit balances on his statement. There were so many noughts on the end of it that it looked like one of those reference numbers from the Gas Board. Or one of those numbers on cheque books that no one knows what they are for, but just consist of rows and rows of noughts.

As I drove home I daydreamed about what I would spend that sort of money on. I just couldn't decide between a Ferrari 456 GTA and an Aston Martin Vantage. But hang on a minute. With that sort of money I could have both and a Range Rover and a Mercedes S Class. Oh, and a Honda for Catherine! Yes it would all be champagne, houses with swimming pools, Concorde to Barbados for the weekend, and Elton John hired to play for my birthday with a select few of my friends. Depression indeed — must have got it wrong.

But now I realise it does not matter who you are, what you do, what your family circumstances are, how much money you have got or wherever life has led you in the past — depression can affect you. Not only can it affect you, it can destroy your life.

I knew it was Tuesday today. Yesterday had been Monday. That was the day I had been admitted. It was fairly basic stuff but I was trying to hold on to my thoughts, trying to orientate myself to my new surroundings. So far I had not ventured outside of my room. I was intent on staying put. The thought of meeting anyone else in the corridor filled me with absolute horror. I was also becoming increasingly concerned about my weight.

It seemed best to just stay in my room and wait for the party to come to me. I was told that Dr. Elaine Mason would be seeing me this morning. It was Dr. Mason that had suggested strongly, I think, that I would benefit from some in-patient treatment. It does not sound bad when you say it like that — does it? The reality was I had an out-patient meeting with Dr. Mason at 9.30 a.m. yesterday morning and I was admitted as an in-patient by early evening.

Again I was questioned about breakfast and I again refused. Eventually a small tray arrived containing some yoghurt and some cereal. I reluctantly ate the yoghurt, checking first that it was fat free. I did not seem to have much idea of time at that stage. I cannot say that time dragged or went quickly; it just seemed to happen. As I tried to interest myself in a magazine, a nurse appeared in my room and told me that Dr. Mason would see me now. I had forced myself to shower and shave and dressed casually in jeans and a T-shirt. The nurse led me to the consulting room.

As we walked along the corridor I was aware of a small hallway, almost a thoroughfare between consulting rooms and the residential part of the hospital. A few sofas and chairs had been squeezed in, and there was a rack of magazines and a hi-fi system. To my horror most of the sofas and chairs were occupied and I quickly came to deduce that the people without name badges were patients. Some people were reading newspapers. Others were chatting together.

What struck me immediately was that contrary to my long held prejudice about mental illness, everybody looked — well — normal. It could have been any crowd from pretty much any scene from public life. It could have been the inside of a McDonalds, the inside of a pub, a cinema queue or your office.

'God, I hope no one speaks to me,' I thought. I decided to suddenly take an interest in my shoes as I staggered past.

Of course my appearance and my ungainly progress did cause attention. At this stage it is worth mentioning that I was very unsteady on my feet. I felt that the floor was moving, rising up to meet me just as the walls swung from side to side. It was just like being drunk, a sensation that I was very familiar with. I had not had a drink for three weeks and this feeling had got worse.

22

Thankfully, nobody did speak to me but it was impossible not to catch people's eyes. They were not looking at me sympathetically; I could not work it out at first but very much later on in my treatment I began to look at other new patients in the same way. It is not sympathy. It is just a recognition; it is like seeing somebody from the same club, maybe someone you do not know that you discover went to the same school as you, and for those football supporters, like discovering that they support the same team as you.

As I was led in to see Dr. Mason I was aware that there seemed to be lots of other people in the room. Dr. Mason got up immediately and came over to greet me at the door. Her greeting had another purpose, to get hold of me and direct me to a seat. This action was done so well and so professionally that it did not occur to me at the time. As I glanced around the room I noticed a male doctor, Dr. Matthew, who had examined me on my admission the previous evening. The other people introduced themselves briefly and took no further part in the discussion that followed.

It was at this stage I understood just how confused I was; although I had sat down, to me the room was still spinning. As I tried to answer questions I realised that my voice was not coming out as intended. I was repeating myself, not in a way that an absent minded friend might repeat a joke to you, but rather like reiterating the last line of a sentence over and over, or a first few words out of mouth over and over, like someone with a bad stutter. Try as I might I could not overcome it, so I gave up speaking and relied on nods of the head. I did manage to ask a couple of questions that seemed uppermost in my injured mind.

Firstly, 'How long am I going to be here?' There was not really a reply to this, just a helpful but vague reference to rest and observation and a number of weeks. Much longer than I thought. I thought I would be home by the weekend.

Secondly I asked, 'What is wrong with me?' Of course I knew the answer to that one.

Dr. Matthew answered that question and explained that the depression had been caused by a number of factors common to everyone: tiredness, stress, anxiety, etc. and whereas for most people they can recognise these traits and take steps to reduce their symptoms, naturally I had not. On a scale of 1 – 10, where 10 would represent the most depressed patients, I was probably an 11 or 12. Not only was I depressed but I was probably alcohol dependent, had difficulty in swallowing for reasons that they would investigate further, and then there were always the feet. I looked away in shame at this point.

He finished off by saying, 'There are a number of reasons why you are here Paul, but I can assure you that you will make a full recovery.' I did not believe him, but staggered back to my room unaided.

Just as I reached the sanctity of my room I heard someone calling, not my name but, 'Hello, I say'.

I looked around and found a friendly looking guy about the same age as me. He introduced himself as Peter and I managed to spit out my name, nodded and looked away.

'I saw you arrive last night' he said, 'How are you settling in?'

I did not answer.

'I have got the dinner menu here,' he said unperturbed. 'Just tick what you want and I will send it down to the kitchen with the rest of them.' I started to feel angry now; this was obviously a conspiracy to make me eat — to become even bigger. As I searched for a way out of this situation, a nurse arrived, again waiting for my answer. Whether she recognized I was in some difficulty or whether she would have said the same thing to any patient as clearly uncommunicative as I was, I don't know but it did offer me a lifeline. I heard the words, 'Would you like to eat in your room tonight?' I immediately and confidently replied, 'Yes.'

I glanced down at the menu being held in front of me, took the pen that was being offered and ticked vegetarian option. I put a line through starter and dessert. This seemed to satisfy my inquisitors. I turned to go into my room. The nurse almost sprinted away and Peter turned and went to walk away. I felt an immense sigh of relief welling up inside of me. He then turned back again and said, 'What are you in for?'

I did not think I would ever hear those words spoken to me. Surely that was a question directed to new prison inmates, and isn't there some unwritten criminal ethics code deemed that you should never ask a fellow prisoner this question? I am sure I saw it once on *Porridge*. Realising that I couldn't not answer I muttered, 'depression' under my breath.

'Oh right, like most of them in here,' he said. 'I'm on the alcohol abuse ward. Been here six weeks. I'm going home on the weekend. If you would like me to show you around, show you the ropes, just give me a shout. I will normally be in 'The Annexe.'

I had no intention of taking up his offer, but must have looked even more confused at this. He pointed back to the group of sofas I had noticed earlier as if to say 'there'. Finally I made it into my room. I would have liked to shut the door but it was still secured back to the wall. What did he mean 'show me the ropes'? I was reminded of all those prisoner of war films I had watched as a kid; you know, *The Great Escape* where the new POW was always interrogated to see if really he was a German spy, before the plans of the escape tunnel were revealed to him. What was there to learn in here? I just wanted to get out as quickly as possible. Maybe he had a point. When I could walk and speak I would be sure to look him up, I thought.

The next thing I remember was a number of patients walking past my room. It was dinnertime. Before I had to face the obstacle of eating something, Catherine arrived with our son Daniel.

I am sure you have been to see a relative or friend in hospital. Isn't it bloody difficult? For most people it is. Catherine can take the whole upsetting and grisly affair in her stride.

For mortals there is firstly the agonising choice of, 'Do I take something'? Normally you choose 'yes' and then what to take? I am just showing off now because I never had to make such decisions. If we went to see someone together in hospital Catherine would make any purchases, buy a card, put my name on it, buy flowers if appropriate, phone ahead to check that the patient was still up to a visit, and arrange car parking if necessary. All I had to do was turn up and most of the time I didn't bother to do that. If I were going to visit someone in hospital on my own, the whole process would be repeated for me in order for me to execute a solo run.

However, when Catherine was in hospital for a minor operation a few years ago I was completely lost. I could not decide what to take her so I just took the children. Did I phone ahead to check that she was OK? No. On arriving on her ward, did I check that she was up to a visit? No. Surely I didn't just barge into her room without knocking with both children? Yes, that is what I did, just as Catherine projectile vomited across the room.

Once Catherine had been cleaned up by the hospital staff I then sat the children on the edge of her bed. Then it becomes even more difficult. You can't say, 'How are you?' I already knew — bloody awful. What did you do today? Well, that is not exactly a rich vein either. Oh, you know, I had a general anaesthetic, had an operation, felt like shit and vomited. What you going to do tomorrow? She was hardly going to say go shopping, run a half marathon, and re-decorate the house or anything else.

Fortunately the decision to take the children with me to Catherine's bedside was the right one. Having been exposed to much more of Catherine's influence than mine over their formative years they were charming, loving and just distracting enough for the whole visit to be a success. I did not have to worry about further visits as by the next evening Catherine was at home dressed in her best clothes, wearing full make-up and doing the ironing.

Catherine had brought me the latest edition of my favourite magazines, *Esquire* and *Top Gear*, and a further supply of fresh clothes including a new pack of three white T-shirts as I was fast running out of plain T-shirts. Catherine had realised most of my T-shirts were declaring an affiliation to a R.A.F or A.T.C. Squadron or some club or event that I may not wish to be reminded of in my present circumstances.

Catherine's understanding and attention to detail — not only thinking of such issues but being able to act on them — is in sharp contrast to my own, as I am sure you will have already gathered. At her bedside with the children Catherine had asked me to bring her some new clothes and underwear for her return home. The next day I dropped them off at the hospital on my way to the office. As I was now eating into valuable office time, I gave the small holdall to the nearest available nurse and asked her to deliver it to Catherine.

Catherine has never said but with hindsight my choice of blue button-through cocktail dress, medium grey stockings, frilly white suspender belt from the very back of her underwear drawer, high heeled shoes and her best going out evening coat, was perhaps not quite appropriate. It did not even occur to me that she might just want something casual to come home in! I was not even there to see her home as I was at the office.

Just to make you feel even more inadequate, Catherine's visits are planned with military precision, last just the right amount of time, express just the right amount of concern and information about what is going on at home (i.e. what Victoria is doing) and just as everyone is starting to get bored and embarrassed, just as quietly and efficiently the visit is terminated. But seriously, I do feel that although Catherine was still wearing her Florida eyes — wide apart and starring — I could see some genuine relief that I was getting the treatment that I needed. Of course, in my eyes, I did not suffer from anything. I thought I was perfectly OK. It was Catherine and the children who suffered much more than me.

Something that I will regret forever and for which I am truly sorry.

But I could not worry about that any longer. Something much worse had just happened. My vegetarian option tea had arrived. 'Christ', I thought, 'will these people never give up?'

CHAPTER THREE
Seroxat

THIN strands of sunlight entering my room awakened me the next morning and I thought to myself that I had made it into my third day. By now I was beginning to understand the daily routine. At 8.00 a.m. my medication would arrive. As it was already 7.30 I decided to get showered and dressed as quickly as I could. As usual, just as you get used to a plan, it changes.

When I was struggling into my jeans, two nurses appeared and looking at my file began to ask me questions about the medication my G.P. had prescribed. As you have already gathered, what I know about medical matters you could have written on the back of a postage stamp and still had room for your name and address!

As it turned out, the mornings were definitely my worst time: confusion, giddiness and difficulty speaking were all at their worst at that time of the morning. Thinking back I must have looked a complete state. Because of the dizziness I decided not to have a shower but just had a shallow bath.

As I can't stand not shaving, and realising I had at least two days growth, I decided I had better do something about it. Then I noticed that in contrast to my room at RAF Cranwell this bathroom did not have a mirror — well, it did but it certainly was not in any convenient place. So I decided to shave by guesswork. Even if you are in full command of all your faculties this is generally not a good idea. By this stage of my illness I was used to people looking at me strangely based on how I appeared or what I said, but I don't think the two nurses were quite ready for the 'Texas Chainsaw Massacre' look that confronted them from the bathroom.

With a concerned expression, I presume for the open wounds on my face, they asked me a few questions about Seroxat. I have no intention of turning this into a medical dictionary but suffice to say that Seroxat is a widely used anti-depressant and I was now on my third week of taking this on the advice of my G.P. I answered their questions as best I could and as quickly as they had arrived they left.

After trying to tidy my face, I decided, as I felt so awful, to lie on my bed and wait for whoever arrived next through my open door.

For reasons that I cannot remember I decided to check for messages on my mobile phone. As the message service clicked on and said, 'You have 28 new messages,' I hit the off button. I don't think I was supposed to have a mobile phone with me; however, my mobile phone doesn't look like one. It looks like a small laptop and therefore had escaped the notice of the hospital staff. In fact one of the nurses asked me why I had brought my own TV remote control with me as that is what she thought it was. Why on earth would you bring your own TV remote control with you?

I suppose this being a psychiatric hospital they get used to all sorts of things that don't make sense. I knew that I couldn't face hearing my colleagues' voices, so I decided to check the text message part of my phone. I had one new message. It was from my colleague and great friend Lester. All it said was, 'Foxy, are you on Seroxat?' I quickly texted back saying, 'Yes, have been for last three weeks.' A message came back immediately from Lester saying, 'Foxy, Seroxat not good.'

Being asked about my medication by the nurses and Lester's text messages were purely coincidental, but in my mind, or least what was left of it, I knew there had to be some form of conspiracy. The same conspiracy that made me eat food I didn't want and hounded me out of my job but before I could worry even more, a nurse called Sheila arrived.

Sheila sat down on the foot of my bed and asked me how I was feeling. Without waiting for a reply she said I seemed very anxious. I mumbled to her about the Seroxat and about the message from my friend. Sheila explained very calmly that there had been a TV programme at the weekend suggesting that Seroxat had given one or two causes for concern but overall considering the millions of prescriptions every year it was still one of the safest anti-depressants on the market. There was something about her calm voice that really appealed to me. I decided I did not know enough about the subject to worry.

Just as I thought that things were getting better and Sheila had come in to ask me how I was, she got up and said, 'Right. If you would just like to follow me Paul, we will get your first blood test out

Paul Fox

of the way.' She could not have had more of an effect on me if she punched me in the face.

'Blood test.' I said. 'Why?'

Sheila said very calmly, 'So that we can monitor how you are doing.'

I absolutely hate having my blood taken. I faint and even after I have come round I still feel faint the rest of the day. Even as I am writing this I'm beginning to feel faint. I thought I could use the same trick that I had used to get me out of being weighed by perhaps telling Sheila what she wanted to know. Sheila just smiled when I began mumbling again. We both understood at the same time that I did not know anything about what was going to happen to me. All I knew was that I did not want a blood test.

For a moment I considered clinging to the bed. You would have thought that Sheila would have become agitated and assertive at this stage but no; she sat down and explained to me why the blood was needed. I tried to explain that I did not care what they needed it for. For all I was concerned they could sell it. How it got from me to their laboratory was what concerned me. Again Sheila was infinitely patient. 'What happened to make you so anxious?'

'Nothing really, I have fainted a few times.' I was anxious. Anxious like I was about everything. Over anxious and concerned about the everyday things of life. Now it was a blood test. Before that it had been Lester's text message. Before that, tea last night and of course there was the over-riding anxiety of another mealtime coming up. Not to mention my work and my weight. I did manage to blurt out that the veins in my arms are difficult to find and the digging about by various nurses had bruised me quite badly in the past. In trying to offer a solution I suggested they take the blood from the veins in my hand which are quite prominent.

Sheila thought for a moment and then said, 'I see no problem and as you are feeling a bit wobbly I'll get the equipment and do it right here.' The blood was out of my hand and in the bottle within the next five minutes and I can honestly say I did not feel a thing. If getting blood out of difficult patients was an Olympic sport Sheila would be a world champion.

Really, I was no stranger to being medically examined. Since the choking incident in Florida I had had regular investigations into

30

why I could not swallow. The doctors tried everything. The American doctor's idea of being allergic to the coating on french fries was quickly dismissed. We then embarked on an elimination diet including wheat, dairy products, gluten. In fact, you name it, I have tried deleting it to improve my digestion and I had had three endoscopies. To save you reaching for your medical dictionary this involves putting a camera down your throat to see what is going on.

When I was first told of the procedure by my consultant, being the world's biggest wimp, I was immediately terrified. I felt better when he said the word 'Theatre.'

'So you mean this will be done in an operating theatre?' I said.

'Oh, yes. Of course,' he replied, as if to say, where did you think I was going to do it, in the car park? He could see that I had my doubts, so he showed me the instrument concerned. It looked like a small hose with a light on the end. A bit like the shower attachment in some posh hotels and the one in our en-suite bathroom (Catherine chose it). Or better still, if you have ever seen the film E.T. it is about the size of E.T.'s finger where he says 'Phone home.'

Bearing in mind I was seeing the specialist because I could not swallow, I presumed that I would be unconscious throughout the procedure due to a general anaesthetic. So I paid little attention to the rest of the details. He had a cancellation for the end of the week and so I agreed to the procedure being done that Friday morning. As he got up to shake my hand he said, 'Of course, you will have someone to bring you in and take you home again, won't you, Paul?'

'Oh, yes, of course,' I said. 'But don't worry. I have had general anaesthetic before.'

He looked slightly confused and said, 'General anaesthetic? There won't be any general anaesthetic, Paul. I will need you to be awake.'

'Awake? '

I couldn't speak through fear. On the operating table trying to swallow a hosepipe with a camera on the end? I couldn't even swallow my food. How on earth was I going to get that down my *throat? I seemed to have a knack of being treated by <u>very</u> patient doctors and consultants and he explained at length that I would be sedated but fully conscious, as I needed to follow his instructions as I swallowed what was now looking like a drainpipe. It was too late to pull out. It had already been booked and he reassured me that I would remember nothing at all of the procedure. To my surprise and relief it was perfectly true. To this day I cannot remember anything after him saying, 'Paul, look this way.'*

All three investigations produced no tangible results. I even had the 'hosepipe' shoved up the other way as well! I can assure you this took some considerable talking into and I am sure that the women reading this will be pleased to know it was administered without anaesthetic or sedation. His only words of reassurance this time were, 'Don't worry, Paul, it is not addictive!'

I was not always a wimp when it came to medical matters. In fact prior to the investigations for the swallowing problem the only time I had been operated on was something I actually volunteered for. A vasectomy! Yes, I had always said to Catherine when our family was complete, i.e. one boy, one girl (you would not expect anything else of Catherine, would you?) I would have a vasectomy. It is a simple, quick, and permanent solution. All very commendable, but it is easy to make such statements when you are years away from it happening. However in 1990, with our family complete, it was time to consider what our options were going to be.

I have never liked those rubber things. I have always thought they were like trying to eat a Mars bar with the wrapper on. Catherine can't take any form of birth control tablet at all and so a vasectomy seemed the obvious answer and I had always said I would have one – hadn't I?

So along I went to the doctor's. We spoke for a while about families, etc., and I said to him that my mind was made up and I wanted to go ahead with it on one condition: that I had a general anaesthetic. 'No problem,' he said. 'When would you like it done?'

'As soon as possible,' I replied, thinking it would be months if not years in advance.

'O.K. Would you consider a cancellation?

'*Yes, certainly.*' What is the difference between, say, November five years from now and July five years from now? I thought.

'*Won't be a second.*' He dashed out of the room and almost instantaneously returned. '*OK,*' he said. '*Friday 9.00 a.m.*'

'*Friday? What? This Friday? You mean the day after tomorrow?*'

'*Yes,*' he said. '*You said a cancellation would be OK, didn't you?*'

'*Yes, but I didn't think it would be that quick.*'

'*Do you want it done or not?*' he said.

'*Yes, yes, of course.*' And so that Friday Catherine left me in the waiting room of our local hospital. I gave my name at reception to the nurse and took a seat amongst the very nervous men sitting with their legs crossed, starring at their shoes. After what seemed like hours a guy dressed very smartly in a blazer and slacks, holding a clipboard, called out a couple of names, ticked their names off, asked them a few questions and asked them to wait. Just as I got back to studying my shoes he said, '*Oh, by the way*' in a very loud voice, '*Who's the one person for the general anaesthetic?*'

Everybody looked up. They all seemed to be looking at me, although I don't know why as I hadn't identified myself at this stage. '*Err, that'll be me,*' I said and stood up.

'*Oh, just a quick word.*' I walked over to him, more embarrassed than I had ever been in my life. '*Can I have your age?*' I told him. '*Your doctor's name and your full address?*' I filled him in as quickly as I could and went to sit down. Just as I was about to sit he said, '*Sorry about this. All a bit short notice. Didn't get all your details from your G.P.*'

As I took my seat I recognized that I was now the source of fascination for everyone instead of their shoes. The guy next to me smirked and I sort of half smiled back. '*Why are you having a general anaesthetic?*' he asked.

How was I going to reply — because I am a complete wimp? I just looked at him. 'Well, I thought it was... procedure. You know the right way to do it.' He seemed to believe me so I continued, a bit more confidently this time. 'Didn't realise all the options actually.' Then very confidently. 'If I had known you could have a, you know, ... anaesthetic?'

'Local' he said filling in my lack of medical knowledge. 'A local anaesthetic.'

'Yes, that's right,' I said. 'If I had known I could have a local anaesthetic I would have said so.' I was very confident now and crossing my legs at the ankles. 'You wait until I see my G.P. I will have a word with him for not filling me in on all the options.' Smiling to myself I thought, 'I had got out of that one quite easily,' until I noticed the guy in front of me with the blazer and clipboard.

'Tell him,' said the guy next to me.

'Tell him? Tell him what?'

'Tell him that you don't want a general anaesthetic.'

Blazer man raised his eyebrows. He looked right at me and said, 'Mr. Fox, we are ready for you. Do you want a general anaesthetic or not?'

'Yes, I do,' I said.

Not satisfied with this humiliation he added, 'Why do you want a general anaesthetic?'

There was no way out this time. 'Because I am a complete wimp,' I replied.

'Yes, that what it says here. Follow me.'

I was soon gowned up and waiting for theatre. It is really like how you imagine it, staring at the lights along the corridor, lying on the trolley. I would not say I was terrified. I had gone way past that. If I had been pushed off the trolley at that stage, I would have bounced down the corridor like a broken Action Man, painted on grin still in place.

Then someone in a gown explained that they were going to make a small incision into my wrist. That is all I heard. Apparently the rest of the explanation is something to do with putting a plastic port in your vein in order to administer the general anaesthetic.

However I was so close to fainting at that stage it was almost rendering the anaesthetic useless. Suddenly I felt my right wrist go cold. I wanted to faint. In fact I tried to faint, but it did not work. Someone else came over and looked at my wrist. I managed to make out, 'Let me have a go.' My wrist went cold again and I felt a sharp stab. The second voice leaned over and said, 'Sorry about this, old boy. Having a bit of trouble getting the port in.'

I then heard the first voice say, 'Yes, got it, anaesthetic coming through now.' Just as I lost consciousness I heard the surgeon say, 'Christ, I could have done it by now.'

I woke up feeling rather pleased with myself. I had done it. I had had a vasectomy as I had always promised. Catherine came to collect me and admitted that she did not expect me to go through with it and expected me back in the house before she had even returned from the hospital. This made me feel even better. At last I had done something that even Catherine could not — well, you know what I mean.

There were no ill effects either. I told all my colleagues at work. It was very simple and quick and all the horror stories were completely untrue. Of course I did not tell them about the general anaesthetic.

Just as I was turning into a vasectomy bore, getting undressed for bed one night, about three or four nights after the vasectomy I noticed something. (If you are having your tea right now I would skip this chapter.) How can I put this delicately? There was blood on my underpants. Not much but it was definitely blood. After a quick inspection with the aid of a mirror, it seemed that the blood had come from the incision. Over the next couple of days it got worse and it got sore. Eventually there was no choice but to go back to the G.P. and show him the damage.

'Ah' he said. 'Quite simple, really. The cord they have sewn you up with has become infected. No one's fault really. These things happen, unfortunately. I will give you a course of penicillin and that will clear it up within a few days. The cord should rot away; if it doesn't come back. I'm afraid the mess will go on for a bit though.' This was the bit that really concerned me.

Catherine had already resorted to soaking and bleaching my pants. If my mother had seen them she would no doubt have accused me of some ungodly act. 'Could he bandage it up for me?'

'There's a much easier solution than that, Paul,' he said. 'Just use some sanitary towels for a few days.'

I felt violated! Catherine and I did not even speak of such things. Obviously I knew of them from television adverts and I am sure Catherine used something but I had certainly never seen anything. In fact you cannot be off knowing about it now when every other advert, especially at teatime, is about them or even the sinful type!

When I eventually got home and told Catherine what I needed to borrow, I thought Catherine was going to have an epileptic fit with laughter. Upstairs in our bedroom with me in the bathroom and Catherine outside the door, the said article was handed in to me and Catherine gave me instructions.

'That's right. Take it out of the packet.' Rustling from me. 'Then take the adhesive strip off, then put it into a sort of U shape and open out the wings. Then place it in your pants and pull them up.' I did all that. It felt very strange, and I did my jeans up and stepped out of the bathroom.

'There you are' said Catherine. 'All very straightforward' and then launched into a speech about how I should have been a woman, suffering, blood etc. Obviously at this stage I switched off.
By the next day, coming home from work, something was definitely not right. I had to gain information from Catherine again. 'What exactly is the problem?' Catherine said, sounding very much like our G.P.

'You know those things on the side?'

'The wings,' Catherine said.

'They don't lie flat.'

Catherine started to look concerned.

'I think the adhesive's on the wrong side so they are sticking to my legs.'

'You are supposed to wrap that bit around your pants.' As though every man knew that!

'Around the gusset.' This is as explicit language as I have ever heard Catherine use.

'Yes, I know, but when I do that the adhesive is next to my legs not my pants. I must have a faulty one.'

It began to dawn on Catherine what I had done. 'When you changed it last night was it easy to take off?' she asked, knowing what the answer would be.

'Change it? I said. I've still got the same one on. You didn't say anything about changing it.'

'When you stuck it to your pants, is that what happened?'

'I don't know,' I said. 'I just shoved it in there and pulled my pants up.'

Catherine started to laugh again. That annoying laugh she laughs when she knows what is going on and I haven't a clue. Here I am in mortal agony, injuring myself and trying to make the best of working with this thing stuck to my private parts and all she can do is laugh. Eventually through the tears of laughter she managed to explain that I had stuck it the wrong way round. Several Paracetamol and some more tears (mine this time) later, I didn't feel quite the expert on vasectomies.

The rest of the morning was taken up with a brief meeting with Dr. Matthew; he explained that my medication was being changed from

Seroxat to something called Effexor. I don't want to sound like Elton John's *Rocket Man* but it was 'all the science I don't understand.' Dr. Ramage also examined my feet again. The bloody stumps of my toenails had congealed and I knew that he was going to ask me how this had happened. Sure enough he started with 'When did this happen?' As I was so ashamed I didn't reply but looked out of the window and said under my breath, 'about two weeks ago.'

'Has this ever happened before, Paul?' he said very calmly as if we were talking about something perfectly normal. And not in reality was a middle-aged man tearing at his own body to release blood.

'No,' I said as firmly as I could. 'No, it hasn't.' Dr. Matthew smiled, wrote something in my file and promised that he would see me again later in the week.

When I returned to my room there was a programme or timetable, like the ones you get at school, placed on my freshly made bed. It was a collection of activities including art therapy, creative writing and various other courses, including something called CBT. I had no idea what that meant.

As the new medication kicked in and mixed with the Seroxat that was in my bloodstream already, I felt like I had flu really — very leaden limbs. I just wanted to go back to bed and stretch out. I decided that this was important; this timetable, this programme was my ticket out of here. Presumably I would have to gain points or perhaps pass an exam or impress the teachers enough for them to release me back to my life. I made myself a cup of coffee in the small kitchen next to my room and headed for the group of sofas that seemed to be the focal point of the ward. There were not many people about and I was beginning to gain a little confidence and even noticed one or two new inmates. I was perceptive enough to realise that the dead-eyed shufflers were the new people.
Whether it was the caffeine hitting the chemical soup that now made up my bloodstream or not — I don't know — but in a rush I decided to grasp the moment, see what was next on the timetable and head off there.

It was art therapy. My heart sank. Thinking back to the times in my life when I had heard the term 'nervous breakdown' I remembered with some horror that my art teacher at school had suffered a nervous breakdown. I don't think I caused it but she did say to me once that in the twenty years she had been teaching she had never come across a pupil with less talent! Blunt and to the point, but then this was a Catholic school, and of course I was well used to that type of approach. As I walked across the courtyard that crisp October morning I remembered my early days at school. In fact I could recall my first day.

The Roman Catholic school system in the mid 1960s had a very simple policy. Basically, it took in bright, eager, enthusiastic five-year-olds, and introduced them to a woman who had never had children, who dressed from head to foot in black, who told them all that they were worthless pieces of shit and at the very best they would live a life of misery for which they would be eternally grateful and if they didn't do exactly what they were told they would spend forever in hell. It was quite a mission statement and when you are five it tends to have quite a profound effect on you, especially when the lessons are backed up with regular beatings. Still, I thought, it didn't do me any harm! (No, my children are not Catholics. They go to normal schools.)

It was then I was introduced to art. I was crap at it even at five. I remember the nun saying to us all, 'Draw a picture of Christ our Saviour.' Christ our Saviour, I thought: Is that the one on the Cross with blood coming out of his hands and feet or is that the one with the long white beard and walking stick? Anyway I just drew what I thought was a mixture of both using as many crayons as I thought necessary. As it was my first day they let me off the beating. But art was never, ever, my strong point.

When I arrived at the art studio across the Courtyard from the main building, I was the only one there. Soon a young girl arrived and I could see from her appearance she was obviously being treated on the anorexia ward. She said, 'Hello' shyly and I decided to sit down at a nearby drawing board in an effort to look sincere and to try and disguise my bulk.

Janne the therapist arrived and introduced herself, and explained that arts and crafts were a way of expressing yourself. There was no judgement. You could draw or make whatever you wanted to. You could use the studio at more or less any time and went on to explain in some detail with some patience why this creative therapy was considered so useful. What immediately struck me was two things; firstly Janne's insistence that there was nothing to achieve.

How would she know when it was working, when I was better? And secondly she emphasised that we were doing this for ourselves, for what we would get out of it. I wouldn't get anything out of it, I hated art. I was only being enthusiastic for her sake. If I couldn't impress her because I had turned up, I certainly wouldn't be able to impress her with any feeble drawings, even if I did resort to Christ with blood or the old one with the beard!

Janne could see that I was confused; well, more confused than I already was. After I had outlined my twisted thoughts she sat me down again and said, 'I think you may have the idea of this type of therapy all wrong. There is no exam. It has nothing to do with your medical treatment. It is a way of you expressing your feelings, in a calm environment. If you do not think you can do it with art, maybe you could do it with creative writing' (the jury is still out on that one!) 'or music therapy.' Or maybe I would benefit from the open therapy, just talking with other people about my illness.

I thanked Janne and headed back across the courtyard to the small group of sofas. No exams, I thought. No hierarchy to ascend to. I would have to re-think my strategy to get out of here. Perhaps I could dig a tunnel!

CHAPTER FOUR
The Wedding

BY NOW, life in The Priory was beginning to settle down to a routine — low fat yoghurt for breakfast served in my room at 7.00 a.m., medication at 8.00 a.m. (now changed to Effexor), lunch at 1 o'clock and dinner at 6.30 p.m. onwards; like breakfast I ate all my meals in my room. In between times there was a round of psychiatrists, and psychotherapists, etc., but I was still not feeling any better.

Maybe you are reading this because you know a lot about mental illness; maybe you are reading it because you want to know more; maybe you are reading it because you want to know how to avoid the traps I fell into. I am not sure that I can help on any of those counts but I will try to explain how I felt at my worst. Do bear in mind that these memories are pretty unreliable and are recounted now only though time and a lot of therapy.

I remember the first time I heard the term 'nervous breakdown.' It was when the singer Judy Garland had been found dead after a very poor performance one night at The London Palladium. I recall watching it on television. My Mum commented on how awful she looked and the fact that she kept on forgetting words.

'She has had a nervous breakdown,' said my Dad. I was about 10 or 11 and I had never heard of this before. What did it actually mean? How in fact did you break down? I knew my Dad's car broke down a lot. Was it the same thing? Being fairly pretentious I asked what it meant. All my Mum would say was, 'It means you're very ill.'

Is that it? Is that how she died? She had the nervous breakdown and then she died. But on the news they were saying it was suicide and I knew what that meant. It was a sin. It meant that you could not be buried in consecrated ground, etc. For once I did not think much more about it. It was a shame she was dead but I did not equate this middle-aged woman with Dorothy in *The Wizard of Oz*.

Since then whenever I have heard the phrase 'nervous breakdown', I have thought, 'What does it mean?' 'Give me more information.'

Even though we do not use the words now because apparently, 'We know much more about mental illness now,' I know all too well what it means.

So I will have a go at trying to explain what it was like at the peak of my illness. However, I am not really the one to ask. Catherine would be a much better judge. She watched me almost self-destruct before her eyes and to my eternal shame, my children also knew all about my illness. The choking incident in Florida was really just the start for them.

Just before I was admitted to The Priory, my days would start like anyone else's; I would wake up, assuming that I had managed to sleep the night before. Sleep has been a problem for years. I am almost a serial insomniac. People would say to me surely you must sleep, and I did but even on the best nights it was only shallow fitful sleep or the unconsciousness that only alcohol can bring. After opening my eyes I would have maybe five or six minutes of gathering my thoughts about the day, what I was doing, where I was going, and who I was seeing.

Then it would hit me all of a sudden like being hit with a thousand e-mails all at once; or suddenly turning on the television full blast, sound and vision, in the dead of night. I am not sure I know what the term sensory overload means but it was as if every nerve in my body from my fingertips to my toes had an electric current running through them. Maybe you have had that feeling when you drink too much coffee, maybe three cups in quick succession, and not very much food. This was like twenty cups of neat espresso coffee; it hit me suddenly in the morning and stayed with me all day.

The next thing to concern me was my weight, worrying if my suit would fit me every morning, hoping not to catch a glimpse of myself in the train window or shiny office block on the way to work. Who was this bloated, pasty-faced individual? Maybe everyone feels like this and I never for one moment felt I was ill; I just had an overwhelming sense of unhappiness.

Then there was the dizziness (are you depressed yet?) not only because I was drinking probably two bottles of wine a day; it was the dizziness that made me feel unsure of my steps. Would the path suddenly move out of my way? I began to hold onto things as I walked, stick to the side of the road or side of a corridor, probably more for reassurance than guidance, and then the overwhelming guilt that came with eating. The almost euphoric sense of relief at making myself sick. Add to this unruly behaviour and sometimes an inability to be able to get out of bed and you are just imaging the start of what I had to deal with before I embarked on any task.

If you had known me at the time, very little of the above would have been apparent to you. To be honest I have always been a bit eccentric and it has been said that I often play to the crowd. But my work-life had evolved into working from various offices, seeing different people perhaps every day and not for very long, so nobody saw me all the time and my behaviour was easy to hide. Naturally, Catherine knew and, before you ask, she tried and tried to do something about it. That's the great thing about depression: the worse it is the less you know about it. As for being a bulimic alcoholic that's just the icing on the cake!

I had not always worried about my weight. During the mid 1980s I used to travel a lot to the United States on business, I loved American food, burgers, fries and those wonderful buffets they have in hotels. Mind you, this did cause a problem on one trip. My secretary had booked me into a hotel called The Hampton Inn — which for some reason always sounds rather rude or is it just me? Anyway this particular hotel on the outskirts of Detroit had a _free_ breakfast buffet served in the foyer every morning.

'Great', I thought, 'I can grab a sticky bun or waffle or whatever before I dash off for my day's appointments'. I was really impressed with American marketing. Why don't we do things like this in the U.K.? Every time I phoned home I mentioned it to Catherine. We stopped referring to the hotel at The Hampton Inn but called it instead 'The Free Buffet Hotel'. Soon it was my preferred choice and I was telling all my friends about the Free Buffet Hotel.

The only problem was I got almost too used to it. One Saturday morning at The Hampton Inn I threw back the curtains in my room and as I overlooked the car park (I always get a premium rate room!) I could not help noticing it was absolutely packed with cars displaying plates from all over America and Canada. You know the ones: Michigan — Great Lakes, Illinois — Land of the Lincoln; Florida — Sunshine State; then the confusing ones like Wyoming – Big Sky State. What does that mean? I can't remember them all now but they include The Show Me State. Show me what?

Anyway there was not a car parking space to be had. Although it was a Saturday and I was still seeing clients, it was expensive to be in the States so I used Saturdays and Sundays to see all the people that I missed during the week or were out of town during my visit. Donning my suit and grabbing my briefcase and my car keys I headed for the foyer and my free breakfast.

When I got there it was packed with people checking in, obvious really, the drivers and passengers of all those cars. Suddenly I thought, 'The weekend. I wonder if they still have the free buffet.' Sure enough, almost ignored in one corner there was the usual array of Cheerio's, bagels and sticky buns. Gulping down in two mouthfuls my cup of coffee and with the reminder of my sticky bun in my hand I headed for my beautiful rented Thunderbird (I up-graded again!)

After several appointments I returned to the Hampton Inn at about 7.00 p.m. that evening and really struggled to find a car parking space. Having virtually touch parked in the space I grabbed my things from the car and headed into the hotel. The foyer was just like I had left it; crammed full of people, but they all had plates, paper plates, and were all eating and drinking. Then it dawned on me not only did they have a free breakfast buffet at weekends, they must have a free evening buffet as well. Everyone looked very smart, nodded and smiled at me and I nodded and smiled back. I noticed a fabulous buffet, you know, in the corner where the sticky buns had been that morning. There was everything: seafood from the Great Lakes, things on sticks, vol-a-vont, salad. 'This is really great', I thought, put my briefcase down, grabbed a plate and dived in. With my plate piled high I grabbed a complimentary glass of — well, it tasted like champagne! This was great value all at $35 a night. I take my hat off to our American cousins. How can they manage to do all this?

While I was steeped in admiration I started to look around. People were still nodding and smiling at me. I was nodding and smiling back. Then I had a vague sense that all was not how it seemed. Of course, I hadn't noticed that not only was everybody dressed up but the ladies were all wearing hats. The men all had buttonholes. There was a large white cake on the buffet. People were still looking at me and I am sure you have got this before I did. Yes, I was at someone's wedding reception!

I was still grinning at everyone. I think they realised at just about the same time I did that I did not belong there. I was wondering how I was going to get myself out of this latest scrap when a large woman came hurtling towards me arms outstretched screeching, 'You came, you came. I said to Brad you would. All the way from Wall Street.'

My grin got even more fixed, this time with fear. Any normal person would have explained the mistake. Not me. I went with it. I was somebody from Wall Street. I did not know what my name was or who Brad was but I did know I was at his wedding. The food was jolly nice! After shaking hands with some very nice people, and listening to a couple of speeches, I managed to find the fire escape and my briefcase and hurtled full pelt for my room.

CHAPTER FIVE
Achtung! Soap

BEING a heavy drinker does have its funny side. You will have already gathered that quite a lot of my job meant that I travelled around dealing with overseas clients. I got more than the odd trip overseas. So I was thrilled when I got the opportunity to speak to some existing and some potentially new clients in Stuttgart, Germany.

Everybody knows what they make in Stuttgart, don't they? In case you are not a fan of Jeremy Clarkson they make one of his favourite sports cars — Porsche. In fact I can't think of anything else they make in Germany apart from sports cars. Oh, yes, I do: cameras apparently. And leather shorts. And for the fashion conscious, Hugo Boss clothes (great if you are fat!) And they do a neat line in European warfare but that is another story.

As I looked at the letter on my desk I felt the excitement grow. 'Would I consider giving a talk about expatriate pension plans to the British workers at the Porsche factory?' Would I consider it? Let me think about that. Yeah, OK. I thought about it and a week later I was on the plane to Stuttgart.

My anxiety and enthusiasm does not allow me to plan business trips very well, I wanted to get to my destination as quickly as possible, especially to the home of Porsche. I wonder if they will give me a discount. I considered my options sitting in the back of a Mercedes taxi on my way to the hotel. If you have not been to Stuttgart, don't worry. You have not missed anything. If you go to Basildon in Essex or Milton Keynes you can have a similar sort of experience. I decided to check into the hotel, which was on the edge of an industrial unit, and go exploring.

As part of a ritual now I always check my wash bag to see if I need to buy anything. I had a nasty experience once which meant that instead of using the tube of toothpaste kindly supplied by Catherine, I used a tube of Germolene which Catherine had packed *for reasons that still escape me, to clean my teeth. Now in my defence I was slightly jet lagged and it was dark but as I brushed the pink liquid round my mouth I thought, 'Christ, what on earth is this toothpaste? I bet it was on special offer.'*

After a brief inspection of my wash bag in Stuttgart I found all was okay in the toothpaste department but perhaps another bar of soap would be a good idea. There must be a supermarket or something nearby and this would be a chance for me to check out my bearings before being picked up at 3.00 p.m. to go to the factory.

I set out in a determined manner for the town centre. It may surprise you to know that despite a fair amount of overseas travel I don't speak any other languages. In fact I only ever resort to raising my voice to people who don't speak English and if that fails, waving my hands in the air or punching them (don't knock it, it seems to work). I have also discovered that you can go anywhere in the world and say' two beers, please' and get exactly what you want.

I walked for quite a distance and just ahead of me I began to notice people parking their cars along the side of the road, and then walking to a large building with rows of flags in front of it. It was a large glass-fronted building and I could make out couples, children, older people going in one door and similar types coming out the other, laden down with carrier bags. You don't have to be a genius to work out this was a supermarket. So I thought I would head on in.

It should have dawned on me fairly early on that even the most exclusive supermarket, even in this most Teutonic area of Germany, would not charge for admission. This one did. As I got up to one of the booths a uniformed henchman said something to me. I just looked at him, shrugged and went to pass. 'Nein' was his response; I didn't have any German to offer back so thought I would inform him of the type of purchase I wanted to make. 'Soap!' That didn't work. So I said it a bit louder with more definition: 'I wish to purchase soap.'

People were beginning to look now. The security guard then rattled off several lines of German. Unfortunately the German language does not sound anything like a language, does it? In fact hearing somebody speak German is exactly the same sound as listening to somebody being sick (my speciality) into a paper bag on an aircraft. I had run out of all my options now. I did the arm-waving bit and even put in a hasty routine of showering and scrubbing under my arms. I was only left with punching him and frankly he was bigger than me, and he had a uniform. We both starred at one another for a while, waiting for something else to happen and fortunately it did.

A guy in a fluorescent jacket and with a walkie-talkie appeared. At last I was saved. A fluorescent jacket and walkie-talkie coming to your rescue is definitely a welcome sight even if you are only trying to purchase soap from an exclusive German supermarket. He glanced at me and looked at the guard. They exchanged sick making sounds with one another and the guy with the fluorescent jacket said, 'English?' I could not resist but replied, 'Yes, of course. How did you guess?'

He said nothing but opened the small gate in front of him which let me in to the supermarket. I nodded and said, 'Thank you' as loudly and graciously as I could and fixed Fritz in the uniform with my filthiest of looks and headed on in.

Guess what? It wasn't a supermarket. There were what looked like trade stands: flying flags from different countries, some wine, some cheese, and people in what must have been the national costume. 'What sort of a bloody supermarket is this?' I said out loud.

People looked round, but then seemed to carry on with what they were doing. At this point I began to curse myself. I had set out earnestly full of intent to purchase a bar of soap; I was now in a building the size of Earls Court, full of Germans at some strange festival.

I began to sweat; I think I have read about this, in the Odessa Files. Perhaps they were going to try and resurrect Hitler. Perhaps I would never make it to the Porsche factory. Perhaps I was here to account for the bombing of Dresden. I decided to make for the exit. Fritz was beginning to eye me as well. I thought I recognised the uniform — Waaffen S.S. (Supermarket Brigade).

48

'Hello, welcome to Stuttgart,' said an extremely attractive twenty-something female to me. Suddenly I forgot about the exit and leapt on (not literally!) this poor unsuspecting English woman. It all came out. I had only just arrived, staying at hotel, talking about pensions, looking for soap, lost, confused, and already had a row. She eyed me with some concern but explained that this was a travel fair; she was part of the English display over in the corner. An annual event apparently in Stuttgart. She gave me a voucher for a complimentary glass of wine at the British Airways stand. 'Fantastic', I said. 'Just one question. Where can I buy some soap?'

I made it back to the hotel, showered (I found some soap packed in my suitcase, a fresh bar. Catherine had anticipated my needs but left out the Germolene.) I made it down to the foyer of the hotel to await the driver from Porsche. I wondered whether they would send a Porsche, might even let me drive.

My hopes were dashed when an untidy, unshaven taxi driver approached me. 'Herr Fox?' 'Yah, er, yes,' I said.

'Porsche now,' pointing to his watch and to the car park to his Mercedes taxi. The fact that I didn't speak German seemed lost on this taxi driver. He just gabbled away, talking about the same things British taxi drivers talk about: the government, the E.U., the price of houses, how crap Gareth Gates is. Did you hear the one about the English guy trying to buy soap at the Travel Fair?

We were soon at the Porsche factory. This was when my anticipation peaked; I had rehearsed my presentation over and over. This was going to be fantastic. We were going to get loads of new clients and I was going to get a massive discount on a Porsche. When I got home they would carry me around in a chair.

I gave my presentation. Not in a show room full of Porsches as I had imagined, but in an anonymous meeting room without a Porsche in sight. But still I was pleased with the outcome. I rattled through my repartee of offshore tax planning opportunities for expatiates, went through a snapshot of today's financial markets and explained the services that my company could offer them. All seemed to go down very well, so well in fact that we all ended up in a bar along the road. And that is when the trouble really started.

After a few beers and now visibly relaxing into my role as international ambassador for the English speaking nations, one of the Germans suggested that I try the local beer. Take it from me, should you ever find yourself in such unlikely circumstances there are two things I can be absolutely certain of in Germany. Firstly, trade fairs don't sell soap and secondly, the local brew is fucking lethal!!!!!

This particular concoction was called Vicenbeer. It came in a jug with lemons floating in it and tasted like lemonade really. Well, like lemonade that is 40% proof. After about three or four pints of that, things started to get a bit hazy, and realising I hadn't eaten since the morning I decided to get something to eat. Having waved my potential clients off at the door and with several appointments organised for the next day I set off for the restaurant.

I couldn't believe the cheek of it. The menu was in German, the waiter did not speak any English and no amount of arm-waving could convey the fact that I was a vegetarian (even before being bulimic I was still bloody fussy!) So I gave that up as a bad job and settled for a couple of packets of crisps and few more Vicenbeers in the bar before heading back to my hotel room in the back of the oldest, rustiest Mercedes I had ever seen.

The next morning I woke up and headed off to my appointments and that afternoon was back on the plane to Heathrow. It was then that I noticed it. Just odd things, really. People looking round, sniffing the air, shrugging their shoulders, whispering together.

I thought no more of it until I got home. Said hello to Catherine and the children. And whilst Victoria and Daniel paraded around the living room in their new Lufthansa T-shirts, Catherine looked at me and said, 'You stink of lemons.' 'It's the German soap,' I said.

As the clocks had changed the evenings were dark and passed relatively quickly. After tea most people would retreat to their rooms to meet with other 'inmates' or have a visit from family or friends, and it seemed to be the etiquette that if you wanted to talk you stayed by the small group of sofas. I was not yet comfortable in my surroundings but I did feel that, as there had been a new intake,

I was sufficiently high enough up the food chain to establish myself on one of the sofas.

Some traditions of British life don't change and so very often people would not talk to one another unless they were introduced. I have often thought how strange this is and almost exclusively a British problem. How many times have you gone to a school Open Evening or Sports Day (not that I ever have) and walking up the road to the school gate see people that you see every day who presumably have the same anxieties and interests as you and are going to enjoy, or at least tolerate a school event, and yet you don't speak? Your children may even be best friends!

But anyway I soon started to say hello to other patients and as I contemplated my position on the sofa for the first time I was at least pleased that I was able to remember some people's names and be on at least nodding acquaintance with everybody else. With a rush of blood and presumably prescription medication to the head, I offered to make the few people closest to me a drink.

Of course me being me and being totally unaware of the 'signs' as Catherine says, I hadn't noticed that the small gathering of sofa people tended to gather at about 7:45 and as it was now ten to eight there were a number of patients milling around in doorways and generally making their way to sofa land.

As I staggered down the corridor to the small kitchen area with an order for 4 cups of hot chocolate plus my own coffee, my seat was soon taken in the increasingly busy hinterland between the ward and the rest of the hospital. What I hadn't understood was that at 8 o'clock those patients that were on additional medication for anxiety or drug addiction were quite keen to obtain their evening fix as soon as possible. With no bar in sight I wondered why people seemed more relaxed later on in the evening.

All of this was still to dawn on me as on arriving at the kitchen area I discovered that I had no idea how to make drinking chocolate. Now you may be reading this thinking how sad, much more of a basket case than you had originally thought. But no, this was not my illness; this was just my general way of life. Should I have ever wanted drinking chocolate at home, Catherine would have made it.

It would have tasted wonderful and I would have enjoyed it. But as to actually making it myself I may as well have just been asked to build a space shuttle out of Meccano. Fortunately, Tina came to my aid and should you find yourself in a similar position the instructions are as follows:

1. Switch kettle on
2. Stand talking for ten minutes, before realising that kettle has no water in it
3. Fill kettle from tap
4. Stand to one side while Tina mops floor from overflowing kettle
5. Get cups ready
6. Stand outside kitchen while Tina sweeps up broken cup
7. Get large catering pack of drinking chocolate powder from cupboard
8. Place one or two teaspoons full of powder in each cup
9. Fill each cup with water from kettle
10. (Optional) Help Tina brush spilt drinking chocolate off her clothing
11. Stir each cup with teaspoon provided (or nearest equivalent)
12. Put cups on to tin tray
13. Hold breath as shock of several tin trays hitting floor sets the adrenaline racing
14. Explain to irate patient in adjacent room what all the noise is about
15. Replace tin trays from floor, to original storage area
16. Return triumphantly to sofa land to claim glory for being such a good sport

That was my first and last time at making everyone a drink.

Now that medication had been administered to those that needed it I set about finding out what happened in open therapy and how I could prepare myself. I didn't get very far. I mistook this lack of information as a possible way of tripping me up or was it that everyone just wasn't used to talking? But if I thought people were reserved or shy I was in for a big shock; because the next morning I started my first group therapy session.

Still not convinced that there was not an exam or points to be scored, I thought I had better try and get some advance information on what goes on. After all we were all there because we were suffering from one form of mental illness or another. As I skulked back to my room that night I consoled myself that it was hardly going to be University Challenge.

After all I had seen Ally McBeal. I knew what therapy was all about. Loads of people sitting on the floor on bean bags blaming their mums and dads for their miserable lives. Or the fact that they didn't get an Action Man for their tenth birthday was the reason they were now an alcoholic, or perhaps even they were knocked senseless by Catholic nuns for not being able to draw a decent picture of God the Father (the one with beard).

After breakfast the next morning, I put on one of the new plain white T- shirts Catherine had bought me (from Asda, multipack). I set off in search of the Resident's Lounge, then went back to my room, and put on a large denim shirt over my T-shirt in order to slim me down (fat chance). As with most meetings I was the first to arrive. I was somewhat disappointed to note that there were no bean bags but a collection of comfortable and expensive chairs and sofas (obviously a theme) and with another habit of mine, I chose the largest and most important looking winged back chair.

By the way, a tip to remember: if like me, you have the fuller figure, the bigger the chair the smaller you look. Same goes for cars and airline seats, but only if someone else is paying. As other people filed into the room I opened my black leather folder, wrote the date and 'open therapy'. I decided I was going to make as many notes as possible and hopefully would make so much progress, so quickly that I would be out by the following day, Saturday. With a bit of luck I could be back at work on Monday.

Perhaps if I rang Catherine now she could take my best suit to be cleaned and as a celebration I would wear my best blue shirt with white collar and cuffs and my favourite Gucci tie. I decided to afford myself my first smile in months. This was going to be a piece of cake. What am I saying, I don't eat cake.

How stunned do you want me to be? Even in the first few chapters I have been stunned, amazed, shocked, disgusted, ashamed. If you hang on a minute I will grab my thesaurus and see what else I could be. Nothing at all I have ever experienced prepared me for the stories that I was hearing. Within the first fifteen minutes I had heard experiences of suffering abuse as a child, ranging from violence to the most deviant type of sexual acts imaginable, to living with a violent husband, being hooked on crack cocaine, trying to come off crack cocaine (I couldn't actually decide which was worse), to people that had had desperate personal tragedies including death of a partner. Later on we would move on to some patients' experiences of trying to commit suicide and harming themselves. I joined in on the last bit.

Not once did I hear anyone blame anyone other than themselves for the situation that they were now in and in almost every case someone else was most definitely to blame. But that is the thing I now realise: that mental illness, drug and alcohol addiction and obsessive personalities feed off one another, and after all, how could I judge? That was not the point of it anyway. The idea was to help one another through shared experiences and whilst I did gain comfort from knowing that other people had had similar problems to me I also felt even more ashamed.

Nothing in my life had ever been as bad; in fact my life was a dream for most people. I had a wonderful job, a beautiful house, and more importantly, a loving family and friends. I had never been out of work, been made redundant or failed to achieve any serious life ambition to date. What on earth was I doing here?

I wasn't smiling anymore and in fact, for the first time for as long as I can remember, my eyes were moist with tears. With disgust and self-loathing I realised they were for me.

There was no visit from Catherine and the children that night and after a thoroughly exhausting day I decided to head for sofa land again and read the papers. I quickly got bored of the daily news of the Paul Burrell trial and whilst indulging in a cup of coffee that Tina had (wisely) made for me, I decided to root through the collection of magazines for something to take my mind off of the day's harrowing session.

Now don't get me wrong. I have always liked ladies' magazines, and now I have got an affinity with sanitary protection. You get an interesting letters' page and there is always the chance of some decent underwear adverts. So flicking through a Cosmopolitan that looked brand new, I was surprised to see an article entitled 'Stan Collymore – My Brush with the Hell of Depression'.

'Someone slipped up,' I thought. 'Aren't they supposed to cut out this sort of thing?' Thinking I had got one up on the warders, I decided to read on.

I have to admit to not being much of a bloke. I am not really into football or any sport really, apart from tennis – especially girls' tennis. Any sport that involves good-looking girls in short skirts flashing their knickers has got to be a good idea. Mind you beach volleyball comes a close second. It was a very good idea to include it in the Olympics (believe it or not). I had heard of Stan Collymore.

There had been an incident in a Paris bar with Ulrika Johnson, his then girlfriend. Apparently he decided that Ulrika should leave the bar and stop flirting, or the other way round, and when she resisted he decided to give her a slap. In fact it was more than a slap as the resulting photographs in the article showed. Sensibly Ulrika decided to end their relationship there and then. It seemed practical to me at that time anyway, the later furore with John Leslie would perhaps show Ulrika in a different light. The short article concentrated on Collymore being interviewed for the magazine and as I read it, I could identify with quite a number of the points that he raised, but one in particular stuck in my mind.

Unlike me, Collymore became aware that he had a problem and needed some help at an early stage in his illness and told a club official. Nothing happened but shortly afterwards he was asked to stay behind after a team meeting. An unidentified club official had said to him, 'Look mate, you're on forty grand a week. You have got a brand new Ferrari, you live in a luxury penthouse and you're shagging Ulrika Johnson. How the fuck can you be depressed?' Not surprisingly he was stuck for words.

The interviewer, with the benefit of hindsight and presumably an expensive medical training, finished off by saying that his answer should have been, 'If a top football player can suffer a heart attack, break a leg or get the flu, he can get clinical depression.'

It seemed to make the day easier to bear.

I put the magazine down and decided to look for something a bit more light-hearted and quickly found what is officially called a T.V. listings' magazine. It had a double page spread of new films that were being released soon. One in particular caught my eye. It was called *8 Mile* and starred foul mouthed, chainsaw juggling, queer bashing, rapper Eminem. He played the role of a kid from a poor district of Detroit making good by becoming a singer (pretty imaginative stuff).

The title of the film refers to 8 Mile Road in Detroit; as you drive from the waterfront area all the roads travelling west to east are numbered from 1 to 25 Mile Road. 8 Mile Road stuck in my mind like a beacon and brought back the events of an afternoon on a business trip to Detroit a few years ago.

As usual I had rented the latest upmarket American sports car that Hertz Rent-a-car owned. My hotel was on Van Dyke and 14 Mile Road. Almost everyone that I had spoken to, at virtually every meeting I went to, had told me about the dangers of driving full stop, let alone driving anything decent into the slum area of Detroit which started at 8 Mile Road.

'DON'T GO BELOW 8 MILE' was the dire warning. 'AND DEFINITELY DON'T GET OUT OF YOUR CAR IF YOU BREAK DOWN. WAIT FOR THE HIGHWAY PATROL TO PICK YOU UP.' This was of course in the days before cell phones were easily obtainable.

But I had been several times before to Detroit and I liked making my way to the Renaissance Centre and the expensive shops that could be found there. I had some time to kill and I hadn't given the Corvette a decent thrash along the interstate. So after a particular tedious business meeting on Big Beaver Road (What a great name! I wished I lived there) I decided to head downtown. I had a great time.

The Corvette was wonderful, the sound of Detroit radio was playing a back-to-back Elton John afternoon (sheer bliss) and I had a very interesting conversation with a girl in an upmarket gents' clothing shop about what Americans call suspenders and what we call suspenders. *After purchasing a few shirts and socks (always good value in America) I pointed the Corvette northbound for the hotel. The Mile Roads ticked by: 5 Mile Road, 6 Mile Road, 7 Mile Road... Soon be out of the badlands. 8 MILE ROAD EXIT LEFT, the sign was screaming.*

'Not a chance', I thought and buried the accelerator with my right foot, cranking up the radio at the same time Elton was just reaching fever pitch with 'Saturday Night's Alright For Fighting' and life didn't get much better. Suddenly there was a loud bang. In an instant this huge sports car was going sideways along my chosen lane. It all seemed to happen in slow motion.

I wrenched the steering wheel the other way and I over corrected and so now I was going the other way sideways. There was a blare of horns, the screech of tyres and surely the next second would mean I would collide with either the concrete barrier next to me or a large eighteen wheel truck in front. I instinctively closed my eyes and screamed while pressing hard on the brake pedal.

After what seemed like ages the car came to a stop, a reluctant stop, on what we would call the hard shoulder. I opened my eyes. I couldn't believe that I hadn't collided with anything at all, but the car was slumped over to one side. I scrambled out of the passenger side of the car and soon found the root of the problem. The driver's side rear tyre had exploded, a classic blow out incident.

Still breathing hard and mindful of my predicament I set about changing the wheel. This was the era before mobile phones and it was also the era before skinny space saving tyres. I quickly found out that the Corvette didn't have a spare wheel and chances are I wouldn't have been able to change it anyway.

I was starting to panic now; perhaps it was the shock of being alive. Staring back at the skid marks on the interstate I was also aware that the hard shoulder of any motorway was a pretty dangerous place to be. The clock was ticking now. I needed to get back to my next appointment and I was consumed with not being late.

Strangely enough that seemed more important than staying alive (pillock). I knew the drill. I knew exactly what to do. It had been drilled into me many times. Don't go below 8 Mile Road. Certainly don't get out of the car. Wait for the Highway Patrol. But how long would they be? I hadn't passed a police car, and I needed to be back at the hotel in twenty minutes. Don't they know who I am? 'I had better wait anyway,' I thought. I will just sit here and wait. After all, what would Catherine say? I resigned myself to a long wait. Three minutes later I was out of the car, walking down the ramp marked 'Last Exit' to 8 Mile.

It wasn't that far. I did get a few funny looks, I must admit. Well, why not, I suppose? How many white businessmen dressed in navy blue pinstriped suits, highly polished black shoes, wearing a Jermyn Street shirt and silk tie carrying a £150 leather briefcase head on into a notorious crime district in the murder capital of the world? But such was the motivation to get to that appointment.

Normally when I tell this story to anyone who knows 8 Mile or comes from Detroit or is even American, they usually strike their forehead with the palm of their hand and say things like, 'Jeez, what are you nuts?' (I am now).

Looking back I wish that the incident had been caught on camera. I managed to find just ahead of me a run down truck stop café. 'They must have a phone,' I thought. I picked my way through the eighteen wheeler Peterbuilt trucks and stumbled into the café. I will never forget the scene in front of me. There must have been about 25 or 30 guys. Most of them sat around the central bar area tucking into enormous trucker sized meals.

Without fail everybody stopped talking and turned around to look at me. Even the television and jukebox were turned off. In front of them I stood glassy eyes, perspiring and looking like a crumpled advert for Aquascutum, as the biggest, blackest and meanest looking truck driver you have ever seen got up from his seat and lumbered over to me.

'I'm dead,' I thought. I'm dead because I'm stupid. What would Catherine say? Doesn't matter now, for in a few seconds I will be dead. As he approached, the tension and silence was too much to

bear and suddenly it all tumbled out. 'My car's broken down, got to get to an appointment, blow out, crapping myself, from England, have wife, one baby, take my money and my credit cards.' All of this was delivered in a shrill-like voice that would have done Maurice Gibb proud.

It didn't stop him coming though. He raised his fist, placed it gently on my shoulder and said, 'Come and grab a coffee, son. We'll help you get wherever you need to go.'

I never did get to thank him or learn his name but I remember 8 Mile.

CHAPTER SIX

F*r*i*e*n*d*s

THE Chelmsford Priory backs onto the main railway line into London's Liverpool Street Station. After eventually getting to sleep one Sunday evening the sound of the commuter trains began to infiltrate the duvet from about 6 o'clock onwards. They were a constant ten-minute reminder that I should be on one of those trains and on my way to my office in Lincoln's Inn. I had cursed the trains so often for being late, overcrowded, smelly, and dirty and yet right now, I would have given anything to have swapped places and been on one.

You can do quite a lot of thinking while you are under the duvet. And I tried to think positively. Why was I so guilty about not being at work? I will try and list the reasons. Firstly, work is what I did. In fact I didn't really do anything else. Secondly, I was letting everybody down. I was letting everyone down at work because they would have to deal with my work along with their own. Thirdly I was letting my family down. After all if I didn't work how were we going to maintain our lifestyle, not to mention our lovely house, cars, etc? And finally, if it was not bad enough to be unable to work, to be off work because of this just added insult to injury.

I now understand that I would have been no use at work. In fact I hadn't been much use at work for the previous year. Trying to think positively I tried to think about getting better, fully fit and resuming and picking up where I had left off. But if you have ever suffered with something like this or known someone who has you will know it is not quite as simple at that.

'Pull yourself together, man,' I could hear an Army drill instructor shouting. But however much I tried I just couldn't. Even getting out from under the duvet seemed pretty terrifying. But I was going to have to, because today I had my first visitor from the office, and in truth I wasn't looking forward to it.

Val, a charming lady, originally from Finland, came into my room after lunch and told me that Sean was at reception. 'Do you want to meet him at reception, or shall I go and get him?'

I was still feeling wobbly, and even more wobbly at the prospect of talking about work with someone as efficient as Sean. Without waiting for my reply, Val said, 'I'll go and get him.'

A few minutes later a phone call from Val confirmed that Sean was waiting for me at sofa land.

Much as I wanted to see Sean and put on a brave face it took all of my self-control to face him. I was also quite frightened. I was sure that he was here to sack me. I could just hear them at the meeting. 'He has been a pain. Now he's ill, so sack him.'

As I stumbled through the ward door separating the stairs from sofa land, it was the only thing on my mind. Soon I discovered, however, that Sean was not here to sack me; just one look at his face told me that. Sean has got an amazing — well, how can I put this? — well, head, really.

Do you remember the advert a few years ago on television for toothbrushes? The cartoon character had a head which opened a full 180 degrees. Sean is like that. When he smiles his face literally lights up and when he laughs out loud, which I am really pleased to say he does often, the top of his head disappears, and all you can see is teeth.

As we greeted one another, I instantly recalled a meeting we had, probably four or five years ago. Sean worked for an insurance company at that stage and I was director of a small but growing firm of financial advisers. My career and confidence were well on the up. We didn't do much business with Sean's company and he was eager to improve the situation, so he invited me to lunch.

In an instant I remembered how much I enjoyed the lunch. We seemed to have a great deal in common and I recall thinking how good it would be to get Sean on board. I didn't know at the time but Sean was thinking the same thing. And a little over two years later Sean did just that.

But as I settled down to the ritual of making a drink, this time without anybody's help, the wave of guilt over not being at work and the absolute and total embarrassment over being on a psychiatric ward hit me again. In fact it was like lying on a blustery English beach with wave after wave hitting me, with no real let up at all. It is almost as if I couldn't think in straight lines, and as I wobbled with two cups of coffee in my hand back to my room to talk, I could see Sean wasn't smiling but looking genuinely concerned.

If there is a textbook way to visit a colleague in The Priory, maybe some handbook somewhere, website even, then Sean had found it. As my memories are still pretty unreliable at this stage, I can't really remember what we spoke about. But I do know that I felt reassured by his visit in a way that was surprising and very touching. Sean's flip top head made an appearance a few times and so did his wonderfully reassuring smile. As I walked with him to the car park he pleaded with me to stop worrying about work, that everything was going to be all right, and everybody just wanted me to get better.

If only I could believe him.

As I walked back to sofa land and the sanctuary of my room, I could hear a mobile phone ringing. I just assumed it was someone else's and stumbled into my room, bouncing off the doorframe as usual. To my amazement it was my phone. I had told so many staff members it was a remote control that I was beginning to believe it myself! If anyone had watched me answer the phone they would have thought it was the first time I had answered a phone in my entire life. I stared at the screen as it came up, 'Call 1 answered', then tentatively placed the phone next to my ear.

'Hello,' I said in the shallowest, most uncertain voice I have ever heard myself come out with. The voice at the other end of the phone was not put off at all by my feeble response. 'Foxy. It's Lester. How you doin', mate?'

What can you say? 'All right?' 'Fine?' 'Pissed off?' 'Fed up?' 'Mentally deranged?' Take your pick. I didn't say anything. This still didn't put Lester off. 'I'm coming to see you tomorrow, 'bout three. I'll give you a bell from the car park... Alright?'

I mumbled my agreement down the phone. Tomorrow at three it was then.

Lester. In truth I don't know where to start. Lester has played such a vital roll in my recovery that I honestly believe I wouldn't have got this far without his assistance. He has been so helpful that really my medical insurance company should have paid him. At the time of writing, I have been off work for just under one year and I have spoken to Lester every day. I am sure you are thinking this is just another touching tale of friendship. That's what friends are for, when you are down. Nothing extraordinary about that. I hope everyone has a friend like Lester.

But really I was the last person on earth that Lester should be concerned about. Let me try and explain. Five years ago Lester and I both worked for medium sized firms, both in the same town. Economies of scale and worsening economic and regulatory environments made perfect sense for our two firms to merge.

Lester was my opposite number in his company; in fact we had had very similar careers. We were both about the same age. Both had the same educational background (poor). We had both been brought up the hard way in financial services, starting first on commission only, and in today's marketing speak, we were both 'client orientated'.

I love all those phrases. Helicopter view. Let me run this past you. Have you a window in your timeframe? I used to think they were great. I used to use them all the time. What a prat!

Lester now tells me that when I was speaking, normally at some conference or another, he and some of my other colleagues invented a game called Bullshit Bingo. Every time I uttered one of my corporate witticisms they would get to score it on a card. I don't know what the bingo phrase was but probably something like, 'the big picture' or 'macro view'. But anyway I just thought they were concentrating on what I had to say!

So we should have hit it off straight away, and we would have done if I had left things to Lester. But I had a different agenda. Instead of seeing Lester as a friend or ally, I saw him immediately as a threat to my position and he began to irritate me from day one. As you have probably gathered, my approach to things is intense. My approach to my career was deadly serious.

Nothing and no one was going to get in my way of getting to the top. I wasn't arrogant on the outside; I managed to keep it fairly well hidden. Only I knew about the things I did to put Lester in a bad light, to undermine him. Not very pleasant reading now, bearing in mind that later Lester would literally become a lifesaver.

In all of this Lester quickly ascertained that I was far from on his side. And we used to have some spectacular rows. He was everything I disliked; he was Essex man personified. Del Boy in suit. A real geezer. In truth of course, he was happy, well balanced and to use yet another marketing phrase, 'had a good work-life balance'. I just saw him as an idle bastard! No way did he work as hard as I did, and yet he produced similar levels of business to me, and his production only went down when I arrived on the scene. I bloody well made sure about that. (Don't worry. He knows all this, and he was well aware of it at the time!)

I did the lot, went through his post before he got it, sabotaged his files — in fact I can sabotage any paperwork just by trying to read it!

About a year into this one sided feud, our then chairman, Richard, called me into his office one day and explained that a client based in Wigan, that Lester had traditionally dealt with, was considering an offer for the sale of their business and as a result would need advice on offshore trusts, something that I specialised in. I could go with Lester the following Monday and Tuesday to assist. The thought of it. Wigan is at least a four hour drive from Chelmsford. I seriously considered going independently perhaps on the train. That wasn't going to be possible, however.

Lester himself had been unwell and as it was July and rather warm Richard suggested that taking his beautiful Jaguar with its air conditioning might make the journey more comfortable for Lester. It was quite a clever ruse knowing that I wouldn't turn down the chance of driving his Jaguar all that way. It would force us to spend some time together.

As we loaded up the car that Monday morning in our car park, things were already off to a fairly bad start. Lester wanted to drive!

To say that Lester and I argued would be an understatement. We constantly sniped at one another, but in the car on the way to Wigan we just had to get on. There was no getting away from one another. An uneasy truce soon developed between us.

We had to make the trip to Wigan several times over the coming months and soon it became something to really look forward to. Lester, however, still made remarks about my erratic driving style. I've basically got two speeds: flat out or stop. So I would be doing a hundred miles an hour in the fast line or 20 miles an hour in the slow lane behind a lorry. Apart from being a pretty poor driver I'm also a rather hopeless passenger and so uptight that I just can't cope with not being in control and tend to grip on to the passenger's seat for my life, whilst doing an almost ballet type manoeuvre with my feet breaking on imaginary pedals.

Part of the uneasy truce deemed that whoever sat in the passenger seat had control of the radio and CD player. So at least Elton would soothe my mind as we pounded along the motorways to the golden metropolis of Wigan!

I am sure I am already building a picture of me being completely useless really at looking after myself and this is no exaggeration. I am. Simple tasks like checking into a hotel, finding my room, finding the dining room, deciding what to have for dinner completely baffled me. Of course with Lester around that was all taken care of. I would be left to concentrate on the job. Lester assumed the role of benevolent bodyguard or babysitter. Lester would do most of the driving, checking into the hotel, finding the dining room, deciding what I was going to eat. If there were a swimming pool at the hotel where we stayed I would normally go for a swim. Lester was only concerned with, as he put it, getting wet on the inside. These were in the days before I was drinking seriously.

We didn't always go to Wigan. Sometimes we went as far afield as Bristol. How we managed to become such good friends I am sure puzzled everyone around us. We had absolutely nothing at all in common.

Naturally, I began to rely totally on Lester. Lester would ensure that everything would run smoothly and I would try and co-operate but inevitably would make things more complicated. I try not to blame myself since I now know it is a genetic imbalance! Take, for example, the following incident that happened on one of our famous trips to Wigan.

We were staying at out favourite hotel, The Haydock Thistle, just along from the famous racecourse. I can't remember exactly what time of year it was but I do recollect it being bitterly cold — so knowing the climatic weather conditions in Wigan it was probably August! We had a routine of having breakfast together then getting our things together and meeting up at the front desk to check out. I normally took much longer than Lester as I brought more luggage with me. I always had spare suits, shirts, ties, shoes, raincoat, overcoat, a couple of pairs of pyjamas, and a world time alarm clock, just in case the world time zone shifted over Wigan. Lester seemed to manage with bringing a spare shirt and a toothbrush. So inevitably Lester tended to hang about the front desk, looking at his watch, waiting for me.

This time unusually it was me waiting at the front desk and I had even ceased the initiative and checked us both out. Lester was still nowhere to be seen, so I decided to be even more efficient (Christ, I was having a good day!) and start de-icing the car. Boy, did it need it. My latest object of desire was covered in a complete ball of ice. I soon set to work spraying and scraping; with engine running and Terry Wogan blasting out of the speakers, life was good. I was looking forward to the appointment and hopefully we could be back on the road home by 4 o'clock, so as not to be too late in — for once.

The night before I had managed to park the car as close as possible to the hotel foyer. There were lots of people milling around that morning, pulling coats across themselves, muttering about the dreadful weather. And everywhere around the car park you could hear scraping. It was then I became aware of a smartly dressed guy carrying what I presumed to be a computer laptop, standing outside the hotel looking at his watch every five seconds, looking up and down the approach road like a demented tennis umpire. He obviously seemed to be in some distress, clearly waiting for someone. I thought no more of it and after loading up the car with my luggage went back into the foyer to meet Lester.

Unusually he still wasn't around so I grabbed a seat by the door and began to scan the morning's papers. Half way through the first headline I became aware of the smartly dressed guy remonstrating with the hotel receptionist. The gist of the argument seemed to be that the smartly dressed guy had ordered a taxi to go into Wigan and it hadn't turned up. He was now running late for an important appointment. The hotel receptionist's version was that she had been manning the desk since 7 o'clock, and all the pre-booked taxis had either left or had guests waiting for them and she had not seen or spoken to him that morning. All of which seemed very odd.

Tempers were certainly getting frayed. At this point, most normal people would have carried on reading the paper. After all it had nothing to do with me if he had or had not booked a taxi. He was not my responsibility. I am sure the hotel would soon organise something to help him out. But we have already established I am not most people. I decided to 'help'.

As the guy stormed away from the desk I intercepted him. 'Excuse me,' I said. 'I couldn't help over-hearing.'

'I'm not surprised,' he spat back at me, then gestured towards the receptionist 'That woman is an idiot.' She glared back at him and me. 'I need to get into Wigan for an urgent appointment and the next taxi won't be here for half an hour.'

'That's what I was just about to say. My colleague and I are going into Wigan in the next couple of minutes. I would be more than happy to give you a lift.'

'Oh, that would be fantastic! Thank you, thank you!' he roared and I thought for one horrible moment he was going to kiss me. He marched swiftly back to the front desk to speak to the receptionist. 'Don't worry about my taxi,' he said.

'I'm not,' she muttered.

'This kind man has offered me a lift and saved my life!' As he grabbed his laptop case and walked back to me Lester appeared with his carrier bag and toothbrush. Looking slightly bewildered as to why this guy was standing talking to me I quickly explained. 'This is, err?'

'John,' he supplied.

'John needs a lift into Wigan and I said we would do the honours.'

Lester didn't seem very happy. In fact he barely acknowledged our smartly dressed hitchhiker, but the three of us headed for the car. I remember that John (if that was his name) head for the front passenger seat and Lester almost barged him out of the way and muttered something like, 'Need to sit in the front. Get sick in the back.' I glared at Lester. How could he be so unfriendly?

As we pulled out of the hotel slip road heading towards Wigan, John started to tell us why it was so important that he got to his meeting on time. He was a member of MI6! He was being chased by his opposite number in the CIA for vital information that he kept on his laptop. He had just flown in that morning from Los Angeles and the satellite communication device that he had secreted about his person had already alerted a secret heavily armed rogue English Police Commander to his whereabouts. He needed to get to his office in Wigan, which was located in the outside toilet of his Aunt's house, in order that he could immobilise his tracking devise and head for Washington (not Tyne and Wear).

As this tale unravelled I became increasingly worried about what Lester was about to say. Not normally backward in coming forward, I was expecting him to say something like, 'What are you talking about, you prat?' But no, fortunately, Lester said nothing, just glared at me as if to say: What on earth have you done?

There was no pause in John's story. He had now decided that instead of going directly to his aunt's outside toilet he wanted to head into Wigan town centre to purchase some essential supplies for his mission to Washington. After all he would need to smarten himself up if he were going to meet The President.

Lester and I nodded in agreement. The town centre was out of our way but after firmly deciding he wanted to go there, I decided to get him to his destination as quickly as possible. I screeched to a halt in a convenient lay-by and said, 'Oh, well, nice to have meet you. Cheerio. Goodbye, goodbye. See you soon.'

Another glare from Lester. John was making no sign of moving however; he hadn't even taken his seatbelt off. His story was still evolving. He wasn't sure if he was going to survive. We might have been followed from the hotel, there may even be agents waiting for him in the shopping centre.

By now I was beginning to panic; in fact I was frightened. Lester had still not said anything at all. But his facial expression said it all. I knew that as soon as we got out of this, if we did, a torrent of abuse would be headed my way for getting us into this situation. 007 in the back started to shrink down into the passenger footwell as he was convinced that he was going to be spotted. Then Lester made his move.

Unlocking the central door locking from his side, Lester said, 'If I were you, mate, I would make a run for it. You see, I think this is a marked car. If you make a run for it they will probably follow us.' John ceased on this as a brilliant idea and swearing undying love to both of us and shaking both our hands, but thankfully not kissing either one of us, he bolted out of the car.

As soon as the door slammed Lester hit the central door-locking button and turned to me and roared, 'DRIVE!'

The wheels didn't stop squealing for a mile!

By the time Wednesday afternoon arrived I was looking forward to seeing Lester but I was also a bit, more than a bit, apprehensive. I hope you have already got a good picture of Lester, a rough diamond with a heart of gold, someone who calls a spade a bleeding shovel! Not someone who stands for any nonsense. How would he react? I was sure he would tell me to pull myself together, put my suit on and get back to work.

As three o'clock approached I decided to wait by reception in order to intercept Lester. I didn't have to wait long. A shower of gravel announced his arrival. A thud of a car door and sound of footsteps marching towards reception meant the Eagle Had Landed. Lester had arrived.

We stood face to face momentarily for about two seconds. I didn't know what to say. I wasn't quite as dizzy or as mumbly as I had been but I still wasn't great. A wrong word at this time from Lester would have been devastating for me. I needn't have worried. Lester gestured to the lady on reception, 'Hello, darling.' She looked rather startled but not entirely displeased. 'I have come to see Foxy, alright?'

The receptionist gathered her composure and said, 'If you could just fill the book in.' Lester picked up the pen from the reception counter, picked up the visitors book in the other hand, and wrote Lester Foreman quickly in the gap for 'name'. I could see him glancing across the other sections, car registration, time in, time out, name of patient, name of patient's doctor, patient's ward, patient's ward number. Without another thought he closed the book and launched it back at the receptionist and said, 'Here you are, darling. You can fill the rest in.'

He grabbed me by the shoulder and said, 'Come on then, Foxy. Where's your room. Have you got Sky?'

As I navigated our way through the rat runs of corridors and wards we came across another patient I instantly recognised as someone new. A new dead-eyed shuffler. Still in his pyjamas. Even worse both of his wrists were bandaged in fresh white dressings from his knuckles to almost his elbow on each arm. God knows what had happened, but he was being led by two doctors. In the narrow corridor between two wards we came face to face and had to shuffle around one another. I felt embarrassed and looked at the floor. Lester looked the guy up and down and almost shouted, 'You alright, mate?'

You couldn't help but laugh, but not then. You might think that this shows Lester to be insensitive to his surroundings, but nothing could be further from the truth. I now know that Lester just worked at being the same as he always was. It seemed that everything and everybody around me had changed. But Lester hadn't.

On arriving in my room most people would sit down quietly and ask how I was. And don't forget I had been brought up on a diet of Catherine's expertly organised visits. But Lester didn't adopt the same approach as Catherine. He launched himself onto my bed, grabbed the remote control and said, 'Where's the porn then? '

Both Sean's and Lester's visits had been the first milestone on the road back to recovery. Sean had expertly managed to dodge my questions about how things were going at the office, was calm, friendly and very re-assuring and has been so on every occasion that I have met him since. Lester's visits just confirmed that he was still a good friend, was expecting me to make a full recovery and reassured me that even though I thought I had gone mad, everything was going to be fine. For his overwhelming confidence in me and his telephone calls and visits on an almost daily basis since then, I am and always will be eternally grateful.

CHAPTER EIGHT
More F*r*i*e*n*d*s

LESTER, however, wasn't my only visitor; Hilary and Nigel also made their way to The Priory. I had worked with Hilary for about two years and as they live close by, our families had become good friends. In some ways I was nervous about seeing them. I just didn't want to say or do anything that would upset our friendship.

Hilary's husband Nigel is a no-nonsense Royal Navy type, having had a long career in submarines. I couldn't for one minute imagine Nigel being that sympathetic. This was just a part of my wild imaginings and nothing could have been further from the truth.

As we sat in my room, or cell, as I had begun to call it, I began a now familiar pattern of looking for reassurance of why I was here, why couldn't I have had some other physical illness that would be easier to explain. Nigel then told me how he felt; he had had pressures in his life. Adjusting to life in Civvy Street after a long career in the Royal Navy hadn't been easy. He had also been made redundant and had prolonged spells of unemployment. Why hadn't he had a breakdown? I kept asking. He had more right to it. Nigel leaned towards me and I remember him saying very clearly, 'No, I didn't have a breakdown, but I have had cancer. We don't get a choice in what happens to us, Paul.'

This really should be a detailed account of the discussions that went on in my room, but in truth I cannot remember things that clearly. I have lost days or parts of days. Whether they will ever come back to me I don't know. I remember Hilary describing to me about the shock of finding out that their young son had been diagnosed with autism and how they had to learn to adapt to a new way of life. I again asked the question, 'How come, with all this pressure on you, why hadn't something like this happened to you?'

Hilary couldn't answer that. But I do remember her saying again that we don't have a choice about things like this and that I would get better. As I worked with Hilary she knew something of the worse excesses of my illness especially with food and alcohol. As I saw them out to the car-park I felt a warm glow of friendship. Had they asked to come and see me I would probably have said 'no'. That would definitely have been another mistake.

My only other visitors apart from Catherine and the children were our old next-door neighbours — Janice and Alan. No, they are not old but I have to refer to them as that because we moved houses, so they are no longer our next door neighbours! We lived next door to Alan and Janice for about ten years and we have remained firm friends with them.

As I was waiting for them to arrive I was trying to think of a time when I have known Alan to be sad, down or upset and I couldn't think of one time, even though he has had his own fair share of employment ups and downs over the years. He has always been smiling, happy, helpful Alan. Janice is almost exactly the same, perhaps with a little more down-to-earth approach than Alan, a bit like Catherine really.

Again the shame and embarrassment of being where I was hung over me during our meeting. But I needn't have worried. Their message was the same. 'Don't worry. Get better and we will see you on the other side of this illness.' As Janice went, I remember her kissing me on the cheek and saying, 'We love and care for you, Paul.' Alan shook me firmly by the hand. He didn't say anything but I could see just by his expression that he was echoing what Janice had said.

As I made my way back to my room avoiding sofa land, I reflected on both Alan and Janice's and Hilary and Nigel's visits. Although I might be a complete and utter wreck I did have some fantastic friends and family. The embarrassment began to subside to be replaced with a feeling of wanting to get better, almost to repay the kindness that I had been shown. These friends had wanted to come and see me regardless of where I was. It didn't matter to them. Had I had a heart attack and been in a normal hospital I would have been just as pleased to see them and maybe the visits would have been without the hangover of embarrassment on my part.

I considered the thought that it was just me that was prejudiced against mental illness. I thanked my lucky stars again that I have such a balanced group of friends and close family. Before I finish this paragraph I must also mention other friends and clients that phoned Catherine, wrote to me, texted me with messages of good will and continue to do so. Not just once but over and over. I cannot adequately express how much this meant to me and still does but it has had a profound effect on me and my recovery. I can't mention you all here but as you will see from the flysheet this book is dedicated to you all.

CHAPTER NINE
Cranwell Bound

SINCE I have been home, a number of people have asked me what life is actually like in The Priory. 'Being in The Priory' is one of those phases that seems to have entered our language. Hardly a week goes by when we don't hear a joke about 'being in The Priory' or a celebrity being checked in (more of that later). Let me try and explain. It is a bit like being in college or university for your brain. One patient described it as 'yoga for the mind'.

The whole atmosphere is very calm, the therapists and nurses have an overall sense of well-being about them and that they are there to help. If all this sounds too cosy, a bit like a Travel Lodge, I can assure you that it isn't. Amongst all this sea of tranquillity it is not unusual to hear people crying, sobbing, screaming and hear of instances of people harming themselves (like I did); and others having to be physically restrained from harming themselves or someone else.

But as I have mentioned before the sitting on beanbags blaming your parents for your life Los Angeles style is a myth. It doesn't exist anymore, if it ever did. Group therapy is probably one of the most helpful sessions that I attended. Listening to others and their problems and perhaps more importantly, their route to The Priory, did really seem to unlock in me the ability to see, at least partially, how I had become this unwell.

You know by now that I am not very good at doing things for myself. But believe it or not there are some things I can do extremely well. I was able to concentrate on goals and achieve them. If you have ever attended a sales conference or an Anthony Robbins type seminar, the message is always that 'goal setting' is the route to success and happiness.

One of my favourite motivational speakers is a guy called Dennis Wheatley who is a speaker for NASA and other large U.S.A. Corporations. He says that the attainment of goals that are important for the individual is the definition of success and fulfilment and he is right. It has taken me until now to realise that I did not have to learn those goal-setting skills. I did them naturally. I did them when I was at school. Pretty much whatever it was that I wanted, I was able to achieve by completely immersing myself in the task.

Dennis Wheatley says imagine standing on the Winners' Podium with the gold medal around your neck. Feel the weight of it. Imagine the view from the Winners' Podium and then work out what you need to achieve to get there. I could do that naturally. I didn't have to try at all so work became my mothership! I loved going to work. I looked at people who were doing jobs that I wanted to do. I saw how they went about their daily business. I saw what they wore. What type of cars they drove. What they spoke about. I was able to take in immense amounts of details and emulate that style.

Long before I could afford the type of house we now live in, I would go to estate agents to look at houses, and get involved in that type of conversation. I was going to achieve my goals; there was no question of it.

This, I now understand, was a tremendous gift. Because I believed in things so much I was also able to make them happen. I was able to speak at conferences as a motivational speaker. So why did it all go wrong?

Obviously, it is a tremendous gift, but it is also a curse. If you are forever concentrating on how good your life is going to be tomorrow you tend to forget about today. I was always working on the next house, car, holiday, client. I was not able to appreciate what I had right now. Don't get me wrong. There is nothing at all wrong about being ambitious but I wasn't just ambitious: I was obsessed.

It worked for a while very well, but if I had a bad day at the office, if something didn't go to my well-rehearsed plan, it would ruin not only my day at the office, but the evening (and everyone else's), and the weekend. Weeks and weeks afterwards, I would still be mulling over the sequence of events in my mind.

People would always say to me, 'Don't work so hard; you need to relax. Get a hobby. Go fishing. Play golf.' I never did. I couldn't see the point. The same goes for gardening and D.I.Y. But I do now wonder if I had been able to relax to clear my mind, whether it would have had any effect on my mental health.

I mentioned earlier the lottery winner who was staying at The Priory, suffering from depression. It was through meeting him that I did eventually get a hobby. Everybody was so pleased that I was now doing something other than just work. Let me explain. As a schoolboy I had been obsessed with joining the Royal Air Force and becoming a pilot. From the age of ten onwards I spoke of virtually nothing else. At the age of eleven, I read Paul Brickhill's wonderful book *Reach for the Sky*, the life of Douglas Bader.

I was able to write copiously at school about such events as The Battle of Britain and 617 Squadron's exploits as the Dambusters and could tell you everything about the Royal Air Force's first supersonic jet fighter, The English Electric Lightning. Also at age eleven I wrote to the Air Force saying I wanted to join and got a very nice letter back from the careers department at R.A.F. Northolt, explaining whilst that they were very pleased that I was interested in joining the Royal Air Force, I would have to be at least 17 and a half; although this was a long time to wait, at 13 ½ I could join the Air Training Corps and become an Air Cadet. I would be issued with a R.A.F. uniform and would be able to spend time at R.A.F. Bases. I just couldn't wait. Sure enough at age 13 ½ exactly I joined 106 Orsett Hundred Air Training Corps in Grays, Essex. I loved it. Every minute. I became more cadet than schoolboy. It was absolutely wonderful.

As to why I didn't join the Royal Air Force would almost make another fair sized book. But suffice to say that I decided to make a career in the Army Air Corps, the flying branch of the Army, and the good news was that I could enlist at 16 not 17 ½. That was fabulous as well. Who wants to be at school when you could be a part of the Air Cavalry? It is almost too painful for me to remember but my Army career was cut short after I suffered an accident during an exercise. For the first time in my life, my health let me down and so I had to re-invent myself as a financial adviser.

The years between coming out of the Army and getting married to Catherine were difficult. Adjusting to life working for one of the country's largest insurance companies in London, the work was boring and repetitive but it did give me a much needed grounding and although I wanted to leave every day I stuck it out through my training. These years also saw the beginning of my eating disorder that didn't really get sorted out until I met Catherine. In those days (the late 70s) anorexia and bulimia were only just being talked about as the slimmer's disease from America that affected teenage girls. Little did I know that it would resurrect itself in my middle age.

Much later on, I got to see John, the lottery winner, when my colleague Keith was on yet another holiday. I ended up going to see him at his house and when I got there I found someone who was not really a typical lottery winner. He seemed quite nervous. The house was far from ostentatious and because he didn't seem to want to talk much I looked around the room and noticed that he had a figure of a Royal Marine Commander on his mantelpiece.

'Were you in the Marines?' I asked, genuinely interested in his reply.

'Yes I was' he said, 'during my National Service.'

'How interesting,' I said. 'My Dad was in the Marines during the war.' That seemed to open the floodgates. I spoke about my Dad's exploits in North Africa and Southern Italy. And I told him about going to Lympstone to do some training with the Marines when I was in the Army.

He then said, 'I have also run an Air Training Corps Squadron.'

'What a coincidence! I was an Air Cadet.' That was it really. Business was almost forgotten about as we talked and talked about the Air Training Corps. The state the cadet force was in. How they much needed reserve officers, otherwise squadrons would be closing. That got me thinking and on the drive back to the office it seemed like the A130 had turned into the road to Damascus. This was the hobby I had been waiting for. I had seen the light. I would rejoin the Air Training Corps as an adult.

For those of you who are not familiar with the Air Training Corps, let me briefly explain. Unlike the Army Cadets and Sea Cadets, the

Air Training Corps is actually part of the host service so in order to become an officer you have to go through the R.A.F. training. Now you might think this is a bit O.T.T. After all, they are just kids, aren't they? Yes and no. Yes, you can still join at 13 ½ and most cadets do. But now you can go right through to age 21 and get your pilot's licence, gliding licence, Duke of Edinburgh Award and go on Outward Bound courses. It is all very serious and rightly so. But after a preliminary meeting with the Air Training Corps, that was what I wanted to do and not only did I want to be a Volunteer Reserve Officer, I wanted to run my own squadron!

That was it; from then on in I was obsessed. I didn't give any thought as to how I was going to fit this into my already demanding workload or my almost non-existent family life. I was obsessed. Now, something should have stopped me. I was looking for a hobby. Something akin to golfing or fishing. Something where I could relax and enjoy myself and the Air Training Corps does offer a perfectly good way of doing this. They suggested I became a civilian instructor where you can join in all the rough and tumble of squadron life but you are not part of the Royal Air Force, and you do not have anywhere near as much responsibility.

That's really what I should have aimed to do and had I done that the chances are I would still be involved with the Air Training Corps today. But I am not. Oh, yes, I did achieve my goals. I always do, remember? But it came at a huge cost.

The first part of becoming an officer meant that I had to qualify as a civilian instructor, so after a couple of weekend courses I was soon lecturing at my local squadron on the history of the R.A.F. After the minimum interval I applied for my commission. Two Commissioning Boards at R.A.F. bases soon followed and in October of 1996 my Commissioning Scroll arrived in the post duly signed by Her Majesty, the Queen. I had it framed and I am looking at it now. I am still immensely proud of receiving The Queen's Commission. It did then and still does mean a lot to me.

But bearing in mind the amount of effort that I put into achieving it, how much it cost me emotionally and the time it took away from my family and children, I would hesitate to recommend it. It isn't just a hobby. It is a full-time part-time job, one that carries huge responsibility and one that requires immense commitment.

I should have been able to see this coming and had I not been so focused on attaining my goal I would have noticed early on that almost nobody I spoke to was in my position. I don't mean this negatively, but it struck me from the start that there were very few professionals involved. It seemed that the higher up the chain you went, the more routine or mundane people's jobs became. Yes, there were exceptions. There was a high-ranking police officer, a bank manager and a couple of people with their own businesses. But they were the exception not the norm. One high-ranking V.R. Officer worked in B & Q. Others worked on service counters in garages or worked in supermarkets, stacking shelves. They lived in council houses, drove old cars. I am not trying to put them down because actually they were doing a better job than me. But it should have been obvious that these people had chosen a way of life. They relied on the additional money from the Royal Air Force, to which all V.R. personnel are entitled, to supplement their wages. They had effectively chosen to have two part-time careers.

I, on the other hand, felt that I could have two full-time careers and that I could be very successful in both of them. Common sense should have made me realise it was going to be impossible. Whether this was just the latest manifestation of my obsessive personality or whether it was the beginning of my illness I will never know.

Soon after the letter from the Queen arrived I would be put to my biggest test, a week-long grilling at R.A.F. Cranwell, including two written exams which not only did I have to attend but pass in order to hang on to my commission. Again most people choose a time when they can take a week off work easily, when they have perhaps had time to study what is required of them at Cranwell to give themselves the best chance of passing without it unduly affecting the rest of their life. Did I consider any of this? Of course not!

Within three weeks I was on my way to Initial Officer Training. The journey itself should have been a metaphor for what was to come.

I had an exceptionally busy week leading up to the course including a trip to the Isle of Wight to see clients. The instructions had arrived from Cranwell and were very comprehensive including details of the course and what was expected. I didn't really get a chance to sit down and study them until the Saturday and I was due at Cranwell the following day. It was early December and as I loaded up the car with just about every piece of R.A.F. kit that I had been issued with (and every piece I had bought that wasn't issued), I was on a high state of alert, totally focused on getting to Cranwell and doing well.

Now as I have said before, we live in Essex. Cranwell is in Lincolnshire near the market town of Sleaford. It is the R.A.F's spiritual home. As I waved goodbye to Catherine and the kids my expectations of myself and in the course were reaching a crescendo and I hadn't even got onto the M11 yet!

As you may know there are strict rules about uniform and all types of clothing at every stage of the day in the armed forces. My notes from Cranwell had highlighted this in bold, whilst not in uniform candidates should wear a lounge suit and tie. So, naturally, that is what I had on. Had I read a bit further than that paragraph or applied some old fashioned common sense I would have known that you did not actually have to arrive wearing a suit. They would expect you to change once you were there. This was the sort of detail that I just blanked out, along with looking at the map to find the best route!

For many years, through business trips up and down the M1, I had noticed a signpost declaring R.A.F. Cranwell, so that is where I headed. It is only now I recognize that I ignored a much easier route via my parents' house in Norfolk where I could have stopped off overnight to break the journey. But never mind.

I imagined I would be there in under an hour. Another thing I hadn't banked on was the weather. It was early December and whilst you could only describe the weather as cold but bright in Chelmsford, the further up the M1 I headed, it began to snow. As the late afternoon sun disappeared the traffic announcements on the car radio became more and more urgent. Words like impassable, motorway closed, and extreme caution were being used, while all around me the traffic started to thin out. The snow was coming at me almost vertically through the inky darkness as I approached the turn for R.A.F. Cranwell; it is a right hand turn across two lanes of the busy M1. The carriageway was already covered with a thin layer of snow and I am sure even in perfect conditions turning right at this junction is a bit challenging, to put it mildly. With conditions the way they were it was almost suicidal.

At the time I had an Audi convertible and it was very sure footed but as I made my dash across the carriageway with the car hitting virgin snow it was definitely touch and go making it up the slip road. That really put me on my metal. I was definitely going to have to concentrate on my driving or else I would put the car in a ditch and that really wasn't part of the plan.

In my naivety (stupidity) I had assumed that R.A.F. Cranwell was just next to the M1 but it wasn't. In fact it was a very long time before I saw another sign. The snow was getting thicker and already there were signs of abandoned cars dotted along the country lanes. The signs for R.A.F. Cranwell were getting reassuringly frequent so I must be getting close.

As I gingerly rounded a bend, however, I came across an accident scene. A convertible B.M.W. was facing the wrong way blocking the road. As the dazed driver re-started the car's engine I noticed some damage to the front of the car. He pulled round me and I lowered my window and asked, 'Is everything alright?'

'I'm OK,' he said, but I'm not sure about them though.' He nodded towards what looked like a V.W. Golf a few yards into an adjacent field. I switched on the hazard lights on the Audi and jumped out. It was freezing, wet and snowing hard. Recklessly I trekked over to the other car. By the time I got there my suit was covered in snow, and I couldn't see out of my glasses.

'Are you all right?' I shouted across the howling gale. I didn't get a reply. A woman with a travel rug wrapped round her just nodded. And then she said, 'We are fine. The police are on their way.'

'I have a car phone,' I said, 'if you want to use it.' They were still a bit of a novelty in those days. I was relieved when she said she didn't and I made it back to the warmth of my car.

I was almost completely soaking wet by the time I arrived at R.A.F. Cranwell. I just didn't seem to notice. I checked in at the guard room and was directed to a new Mess. The first one to be built in some time at Cranwell and this was its first week of opening. 'Fantastic,' I thought. 'Piece of history as well.'

Daedalus Mess wasn't exactly imposing, almost a sort of upmarket Travel Lodge. The snow was coming down so hard now it was difficult to see the signs so I parked right outside the entrance.

As soon as I made it inside into the warmth of the foyer it began to hit me that perhaps not only had I arrived too soon for this course, but also perhaps the R.A.F. had opened Daedalus Mess too soon. The builders were still finishing off the dining room. The carpet was still being laid. And rather irritatingly for a building with more than 150 bedrooms, there were no numbers on the bedroom doors. No directions and worst of all, everything looked the same. But I wasn't going to be put off, doing several relays to the car to get all my kit in and asking four times for directions to my room (on the fourth time I was asked, 'You're not on the navigator's course, are you?') I changed out of my wet suit into a dry one and headed for the pre-course cocktail party.

The journey, the snow, the anticipation and my high state of expectation led me to a frenzy of anxiety. As I headed back to my room, the room now so familiar to me here in The Priory, I realised what I needed was a good rest. What I had in front of me was a fortnight's course crammed into a week; getting up at the latest at 5 o'clock and not getting to bed until at least 1 o'clock after homework, endlessly polishing shoes and pressing kit.

It was tremendously enjoyable. Not easy, but I gained a real sense of achievement. I put so much effort into it that I arrived home completely drained and was soon off work for a week with the flu.

It should have been clear to me then that I should slow down. This was a hobby. Had I failed the course, what would have happened to me? Nothing. I would have just had to re-apply. It would have been disappointing; nothing more. Instead I passed the exams and on the final day stepped on to the parade ground as a fully-fledged V.R. Officer. The icing on the cake was the Red Arrows, who by sheer coincidence did a fly past at the same time.

This was fabulous, a hobby I could be successful in also. I just couldn't wait to get stuck into my new duties. Just a shame that the Priory had to go and get the same builder.

CHAPTER TEN
Celebrity

BEING 'in The Priory' is often associated with the Show Business world. There have been countless household names, sportsmen, actors, even minor Royals that have spent time in The Priory. The media laps up the news and having spent time in The Priory is almost like a coming-of-age for many aspiring soap actors and actresses.

So it was no surprise that during my stay I found the room opposite mine occupied by a celebrity. If you thumbed through to this chapter in the hope that I will reveal who it is, then you are going to be disappointed. I could quite easily give you the name but I would not be able to shed any more light on their condition than the newspapers and indeed the celebrities themselves have already stated.

So what would be the point really? Because my task is not to write about them. That has, as I have already said, been well documented. What I am going to ask you to do is imagine your favourite actor, actress, sportsman, politician, soap star, Royal or rock star in hospital with you. How would you treat them? Would you ask for their autograph? It is a very unusual position to be in and I am pleased to say that my experience of spending some time with a very well-known household name was, for me at least, positive.

It was a Sunday evening at sofa land and by now I was well into my stay. I knew where to steal all the Sunday papers from and the routine of skeleton staff at the weekends was beginning to be actually quite refreshing from the frantic to-ings and fro-ings of tests, therapy and visitors during the week. I was first aware that something was different about this Sunday as there seemed to be an extraordinary number of cars pulling in to the car park. It is normally quite deserted at the weekend apart from the staff cars and the odd visitor.

But as I went for my early evening wander (stagger) around I happened to notice that the car park was choc-a-block. All expensive stuff as well, big S Class Mercedes, four wheel drives, BMWs, even a Maserati. It wasn't that unusual. The doctors drive all that sort of stuff — this was private after all! I am glad to know they spend their money wisely.

Anyway, I didn't think anything more of it and on returning to sofa land, found that Chelmer Ward had got its own visitor from the neighbouring anorexic ward. We always referred to it as the anorexic ward as 90% of the patients there were obviously that, quite obviously just that. But there were over-eaters, too. It must have been a cruel irony for one patient who tipped the scales at a staggering 32 stone to be known as so-and-so from the anorexia ward.

Our visitor was Lavinia. I never asked her why, but she seemed to drift over to our sofa land rather than sit with her ward. I thought at first it was because the average age in the breakdown ward was much higher than that in the anorexia ward. Or maybe Lavinia was just stretching her legs.

The eating disorder ward has a very, very strict regime. The patients are not allowed to move after they have eaten. They are chaperoned everywhere and they have to earn the right to leave the ward, have visitors and certainly to go anywhere outside of the hospital. As Lavinia was nearing the end of her treatment she was pretty much given a free rein.

In choosing one word to describe Lavinia only one comes to mind, I am afraid — posh. Not annoyingly. She certainly wasn't pretentious at all. Only the eagle-eyed would notice the real Rolex (a 16th birthday present), the Harrods Account Card, expensive jewellery, and rather charmingly questions like 'What's a bus?' when a patient would be trying to explain to her the best way into town. I remember vividly one hilarious exchange when a new patient asked Lavinia what her father did for a living.

Reluctantly after a while and after being pressed on the subject, she said, 'He's a civil servant.'

'So am I,' came the gleeful reply.

'What grade is he?' I tried to give a look that said, 'Don't go there.'

But reluctantly she replied, 'He is an Ambassador.'

In the silence that followed all I could think to ask was, 'Do they really hand out those Ferro Rocher chocolates at the reception?' Lavinia just narrowed her eyes at me.

So Lavinia-baiting became quite good sport really. I must say she was extremely good company but that she did let slip one day that at her posh boarding school she was forced to learn to play the piano and as I have already mentioned The Priory has a wonderful drawing room in the old part of the house with a full size piano. So that was it. Her fate was sealed.

'Let's get a concert organised.' I felt like Cliff Richard really. It was one of those, 'Let's do the show right here' moments.

'I'm not that good,' she said.

So that was it. That evening's walk round was cancelled and Lavinia was going to give an impromptu performance in the drawing room at 7.30. Just beforehand a few other patients and I descended on the drawing room like Pickford's Removal men arranging furniture around concert style. A little later to protests of 'I don't know why you have gone to all this bother. I'm really not that good, not worth listening to,' Lavinia took her place at the piano and began. She was absolutely fantastic. She introduced each piece, and I don't think I will ever forget the sound of the piano being played so well and filling the room. Everybody was stunned. Just as she was coming to an end there was a commotion. I got up to look round and noticed the room filling up from the door out into the main hospital. This was unusual as on Sunday it was usually locked. Two or three people came into the room, just as Lavinia was throwing herself at the keys in a final flourish and then suddenly, larger than life there he was.

A genuine, solid gold, celebrity. Somebody that everybody in the U.K. would know instantly.

So what to do? Lavinia was finished and there were shouts of more, well done and a big round of applause and then a sort of pause. You know those pauses that seem to go on a long time — a bit like the pause when Lester arrived to see me on the first occasion at The Priory. I think it was Lavinia or someone from her ward who said, 'How about the first piece again?' And off she went again. We all sat in silence looking at one another with our household name in the back row.

News spread like wildfire. By the time we all got back to our respective wards, news of the celebrity had reached sofa land. Why was he here? What ward would he go on? Would the media descend us on?

The answers to some of those questions were soon answered when he turned up; with a few hangers-on. He did not sit down on one of the sofas but after a while just perched on one of the arms. This will be interesting, I thought. Does household name status mean you go straight to the top of the pecking order in sofa land? Would stretching out across three seats of the main sofa like I tended to do be possible? Like most new dead-eyed shufflers, he seemed to immediately understand the dynamics of where to sit.

I couldn't say that he stopped or started the conversation really, and pretty much from that moment on we got used to having him around. The rest of the evening was devoted to the normal routine. Night-time medication was distributed and everyone started to settle-down. I had even taken to changing into my pyjamas and dressing gown early and wandering about a bit like Hugh Hefner.

As I got up to my room on the top floor to settle down for the night, there was more commotion. It seems our celebrity was moving in straight to the top floor. That would never do. What about 15 minute obs.? What about earning the right to be upstairs? What about being one of the big boys soon to be packed off home, having taken their medication and scored at all the therapy? No, this would never do at all.

I don't know who the people were — the hangers-on — but there seemed to be plenty. I suppose that is the thing about being a celebrity. You don't move without an army of drivers, P.R. consultants or security, but I did wonder if they would be spending time in therapy with him. As I made it to my room and started to settle-down for the night, thanks to the sleeping tablet I had just been given, I was aware of, well, I can only describe it as banging and crashing about and some raised voices.

What should I do? Go out and see what all the commotion was about — I would normally. Why shouldn't I now? So dressing gown back on, I gingerly opened my door. This time there was no one to be seen except the wardrobe and the bed from the celebrity's room — I assumed — was out in the corridor. Perhaps he liked sleeping on the floor. Or perhaps the orthopaedic type bed that was out in the corridor was needed for someone else.

But with the effects of Zopiclone beginning to hit me I headed back into my room and was soon asleep.

I wasn't used to waking up in the night, not since I had been on this medication, and it was a real treat, since all of my adult life I have had trouble sleeping. No sleep. Trouble getting off to sleep. Waking early. I could go two or even three nights without any sleep at all. Thus, my new found blissful nights' sleep were a real treat. I was annoyed to be woken at half past two in the morning by a sound that I thought was one of the doctors bringing his Ferrari into the corridor and starting it up. Or maybe The Priory had come under attack or that we were in the middle of a hurricane. I was then aware that this sound had an in and out pattern to it and if this were a cartoon you would see a drawing of me in bed and the duvet and the curtains and pretty much everything else in the room being sucked towards the door and then blown back into place.

You've guessed it. It was our resident celebrity snoring. Now I knew why he was upstairs — to annoy me. I would certainly take it up with him in the morning. Celebrity or no celebrity. In fact I was tempted to use my R.A.F. training to silence snorers. Go into their room. Switch the light on. And hit them as hard as you can across the head. It does work. Try it. But eventually I decided against it. Grudgingly, I slipped back into chemically induced sleep.

By the time I got to sofa land next morning, on my way to music therapy, everyone was asking me whether I had managed to get the papers. As I have said before I was able to ferret them out. I am sure The Priory has got a system for making sure each ward had a number of newspapers. But with Chelmer Ward being at the end of the corridor, they never seemed to filter down that far. So if you are unfortunate enough to be reading this in The Priory at the moment I will pass on my tips.

Firstly, go to reception, and say you haven't got the papers for your ward. You will normally get the answer, 'They have been taken.' Stand your ground. Normally, one or two will be handed to you from under the reception desk. If the receptionist is not around, help yourself. If the receptionist stands her ground as well and insists she hasn't got any, head upstairs into the out-patients' waiting room. No need for any formalities here. They are so nervous waiting for their consultants, they don't care who you are. You can help yourself to whatever you like, especially if you are still wearing your pyjamas.

If all else fails walk across the courtyard to the day hospital and ask the source of all knowledge — Karen on reception. And if even that fails head for the consultants' waiting rooms. Be careful with this one because they probably bought the papers themselves!

Anyway after scavenging I managed to find a complete set of the morning's papers and brought them back to sofa land. Every single paper was full of the news of our celebrity being admitted. The staff said nothing at all. I was *frankly* amazed how cool they played it. There was no censorship. Quite rightly, no discussion. No sensationalism. It was a real testament to their professionalism. By mid morning life was back to normal. Everyone was on first name terms with our celeb. There was nothing to say. He was there for a reason like the rest of us. So sorry, no scandal.

We did talk. Quite a bit especially on the first night and the following afternoon but I am not holding anything back. I can't remember what we spoke about and really I am not that much of a reliable witness. Some of the things he said did not make sense to me but equally how can I be sure I was making sense at this stage?

The newspapers also ran a story about him trashing his room at The Priory. This was a blatant lie. Whoever it was that leaked this information to the newspapers got it totally wrong. I can only assume that they witnessed the banging and crashing about which was just the movement of furniture. Not unless they mistook his snoring for the sound of serious damage to masonry. Like me he tended to leave his door open most of the time. I could see into his room every time I returned to my room, it certainly wasn't trashed. Who spoke to the press? I can assure you it wasn't me. I can be equally sure it wasn't any of the other patients or the staff. But who exactly were all the people he arrived with?

As the day rolled on, stories were circulating about photographers camped out at the end of the drive trying to get photographs over the hedge. By this stage I had decided to do something positive about my vast bulk and had started on a get fit campaign. I decided to jog around The Priory grounds. When I say jog I mean stagger. You know the sort of thing: 20 years of running, 100 yards of staggering, and a sit down with a Kit Kat in between.

Today I decided to go out early and sure enough there they were. The ubiquitous four wheel drives with blacked out windows: a guaranteed way to draw attention to yourself and quite a few middle-aged hacks with cameras and laptops milling around smoking. Some of them even had fleeces with *Sky News* emblazoned across the backs of them.

The only time they seemed to be stirred into any sort of activity was when a car pulled into the slip road. There would be lots of clicking and flashing. This was the only cause for concern I had. Lester (the eagle) was due to come and see me at 3.30, and with his super British saloon car with its private number plate he would be a source of interest. With Lester's ability to have recurring foot and mouth I thought I had better give him a warning that the world's news were camped out and to keep his head down and not answer any questions.

As 3.30 drew closer I thought I had better wait outside for him. Normally Lester's arrival is obvious. Firstly there is a squeal of tyres outside The Priory as he decides at the last minute to turn into the slip road. Then there is the sound of the V6 engine being revved to within an inch of its life, and then the ping of shingle ricocheting off trees, windows, and other cars as Lester slides to a halt. Today, however, was very different. I was gradually aware of a car moving at about the speed of a milk float with a dodgy tyre up the drive. The driver was frantically looking left and right and occasionally glancing in his mirror. What I could see of the world's media was just busily chain smoking and talking on mobile phones. As this steady driver pulled up next to me, I could see it was Lester.

Not the usual Lester. Smart but slightly dishevelled. Unless I am very, very much mistaken Lester had been to the hairdressers! He had got his best suit on and his best shirt and Armani tie. And his highly polished church shoes. Ignoring most of the formalities like 'How are you?', Lester got out. Looking over my head and back over his shoulder he said, 'Where are they then?'

'Who?' I replied, as if I didn't know.

'The paparazzi.'

'They're on the drive.'

'They didn't stop me.'

'They're not supposed to stop you. That's why I rang. And why have you had your hair done?'

'I haven't.'

'Yes, you have. You thought you were going to be on *Sky News*.'

'Piss off, Foxy.'

So that was pretty much it really. I didn't see much of our celebrity after that and since writing this piece it seems that his condition deteriorated to such an extent that he was sectioned under the Mental Health Act and went into a NHS hospital.

A household name suffering from depression is not new, but it brought home to me again how much this illness affects people from different backgrounds and life experiences.

It does not discriminate between rich and poor or religious or ethnic backgrounds but it can destroy your life and the lives of those round you.

Hopefully the high profile of this individual will go some way to reverse the enormous prejudice against people with mental health problems. But just maybe if he had been left alone to get the treatment he needed, he may not have ended up being sectioned.

He has recently been on *News at Ten* telling the world he is fine. I sincerely hope he is, but I can't help feeling that he has made a remarkably rapid recovery.

Know what I mean?

CHAPTER ELEVEN
Rachael

SINCE I have been at home and trying to write this diary I have been using the Internet a lot to find out more about what's happened to me, and what's happened to other people. There are a lot of sites regarding eating disorders particularly. Some of them are very useful and interesting and some of them not so.

While surfing the Internet the other day I saw something that was quite horrific and in fact it was mentioned on television and in the newspapers this week. It was a site that hopefully by the time you read this will have been banned. It was extolling the virtues of being anorexic. I understand that they are called 'ana' sites and they advise people how to choose anorexia as a lifestyle. How you could get it, how you could starve yourself, or abuse laxatives. It has photographs and diets, if you can call them that, and I can tell you it was truly horrifying.

As I have said before, I am not qualified to talk about anorexia or bulimia or in fact any other issue of mental health. I was just a patient. What I had was an eating disorder linked to depression. That has been explained to me and I understand that. My eating disorder has been with me for a very long time, certainly since my mid teenage years, and even recently I was reminded, by an old school friend that I met and hadn't seen for thirty years, of the way I used to pick my school meals on the basis I was only eating red things that day or green things. That might not be too bad but once you start trying to choose food on the basis of a blue colour then you have got problems. It effectively meant that I didn't eat anything.

My brush with an eating disorder led me to try and find out more about it and during my time at The Priory I went to many therapy sessions, as you have already read. I found them useful and as these sessions are open to anyone as an in-patient, patients with different problems would come together. It was during one such session that the real horror of anorexia started to unfold. As I made my way to the main lounge and found my favourite corner I noticed that there were quite a number of patients coming in from the anorexia ward. Some so thin they were barely more than skeletons.

The combination of drugs that I was taking at the time started to make me feel rather sleepy and to be honest I cannot recall what subject we kicked off with. I remember that the lady taking the session, Anne, had a way of speaking that really brought me out of my slumber and made me to start to listen to one particular lady that was talking.

It was a woman's voice coming from my right-hand side and because of the wing of the chair and the acute angle at which I was sitting, I couldn't see immediately who was speaking at this stage. The voice intrigued me. It was the sort of voice you could listen to. The sort of voice that you might hear reading the news. A deep confident, upmarket voice that you might even hear on the radio advertising cars or telling you that someday all watches would be made this way.

As I began to listen more intently, the voice told me that she was coming to the end of her stay in The Priory and was looking forward to re-starting her life. I leaned forward in the chair and tried not to make it too obvious that I was looking at her. I saw the person speaking was a young woman but not a teenager like the majority of the people on the anorexia ward, but someone perhaps in her early thirties. Someone who by normal standards would be described as thin but she was not a walking skeleton or a dead-eyed shuffler. The voice was of someone confident and I thought for a time that perhaps this was a member of staff or maybe a relative talking about someone else. I couldn't equate this self-assured young woman to anyone else in the room. She seemed like she didn't belong there.

The voice belonged to Rachael and a number of the things she said struck a chord with me. She spoke about her wariness of food at the beginning of her illness and accepting that she had become ill for whatever reason. She explained that she had received treatment and was now looking forward to re-starting her life. I hoped that in the not too distant future I would be saying the same thing.

We got into the pattern of Rachael speaking and then me speaking in the group, then Rachael, then me. It seemed as if everything she said applied to me personally, even though by now I knew that my disorder was just that, and compared to what Rachael had suffered it had just been a walk in the park, just a brush with an eating disorder.

The hour session seemed to fly by and soon people were picking up the papers and forming into small groups or drifting back to their wards. Rachael and I began to talk naturally, and so over a cup of coffee in Lavinia's music room, otherwise known at the reception lounge, her story began to unfold.

The voice told me that seven years prior to being admitted to The Priory she had been off work for six months having been diagnosed with M.E. As Rachael reached for a sip of coffee I interrupted her. It is a habit of mine. I don't know why but I always seem to want to know what people do for a living. I suppose it is a hangover from a military education to somehow find out what rank other people are. It is a useless trait and it irritates the hell out of Catherine. I have noticed it in other men, too, and it is a habit I do hope I can kick.

However, unfazed, she immediately replied that she was a qualified chartered accountant and had worked as an auditor for a large firm. A firm that I knew of. She also told me that she had worked in the classical music business both as a French horn player and as an orchestral manager. Her rank confirmed, I turned my attention to my coffee and settled further back in my chair.

She had begun to feel ill during a particularly stressful time at work. Rather than feeling better when the pressure of work decreased she began to feel worse and worse, eventually being diagnosed with M.E. (sometimes known as chronic fatigue syndrome). Rachael was advised to take time off work and let her body mend itself. During her recovery period she suspected that certain foods were making her feel physically worse, so she began to keep a food diary, not in itself anything unusual. And in fact common practice for people suffering fom M.E. She then began to exclude certain foods from her diet, believing wrongly that they were perpetuating her illness. She and her husband then moved from Cheshire to a five hundred year old former Manor House in Norfolk that needed considerable renovation. Once she felt physically improved, Rachael took on the project of renovating the house full time rather than return to her previous career.

Although the symptoms of M.E. gradually improved she was now excluding more and more foods, fearing her illness and particularly vomiting. She told me she had a phobic fear of vomiting since she was a child and she could not understand my gaining pleasure from making myself sick, because it was not something she could ever contemplate doing herself.

At this time she was also beginning to show signs of obsessive compulsive disorder (OCD), being especially afraid of germs being present when she was preparing or eating food since these might make her vomit. OCD rituals and an increasing fear of food meant she continued to eliminate food from her diet and thus lost increasing amounts of weight.

Her family and friends began to notice her weight loss and at first, like me, people always praise you for losing weight. It is strange, isn't it?

Surely drastic weight loss is a sign that something is wrong, if not with your body, certainly with your head. But that's the way it is. It is just what happens; you lose weight, you look good and people praise you.

Just to try to put this into perspective, Rachael is 5'6" tall and prior to her self imposed diet and food exclusion regime, she was 9 and half stone and wore a dress size 12, less than a year later she was 8 and half stone, and then 8 stone. Still not too drastic I hear you say, but her fear of vomiting exacerbated her fear of food, her OCD rituals became more and more difficult to control or hide, and slowly she was sliding into the jaws of a killer illness. The more weight she lost the more irrational she became about food, her weight and germs. Rachael was not longer in control and she was no longer a Chartered Accountant or a house renovator, she had a new career ... anorexia.

Once her weight got below 8 stone, her periods stopped. It was then that the alarm bells began to ring. She rang the Eating Disorders Association in Norwich. She told them about her fear of vomiting and embarked on a course of counselling which lasted for a further year. Two years before admission to The Priory she had a bone scan and was told that she had reduced bone density and finally later on in the same year she was at last diagnosed with anorexia. She was alarmed but she looked upon her diagnosis as a licence not to eat. So far from being the beginning of the end of her story it wasn't even the end of the beginning.

After a three month period, the following year Rachael's weight plummeted to a life threatening 5 stone. As I sat riveted to my chair while I and my coffee went cold, Rachael said, 'I need to show you something', and reached into her shoulder bag and pulled out a photograph. The photograph was of a woman. There was no colour in the photo and in the soft lighting of the lounge it looked almost sepia.

It was a photo of a pensioner, a woman in her late maybe seventies or eighties. So thin that her cheek bones protruded and the skin hung from her face, making her eyes sink into her skull. Her neck muscles and collarbone were horribly exposed and she was literally skin and bone. It reminded me of the photographs I had seen as a schoolboy of the horrific experiments at Auschwitz or Belsen. The people there were literally walking skeletons and this was a photo with that amount of impact. As I am sure you will realise the photo was of Rachael on the day that she was admitted to The Priory.

Are you still interested in having anorexia as a lifestyle? Perhaps you should know what happens to anorexics in The Priory.

At the time of her admission Rachael's bones were in danger of breaking through the papery thin layer of skin that was her only covering and so she had to lie on an inflatable mattress that rippled underneath her every couple of minutes. She had to lie on one side or the other to protect her sacrum. Nurses would come in at regular intervals day and night to turn her over to make sure she had not strayed over onto her back. A pillow was placed between her legs to prevent the bones in her knees from grating painfully against one another.

One of the first tests that The Priory did was a blood test and she was told that her potassium levels were dangerously low. This didn't mean much to me but Rachael explained that without potassium you are at high risk of having a heart attack. My mind went straight back to the news of Karen Carpenter and her battle with anorexia that ended not through lack of food but through heart attack.

They were so worried that Rachael might have a heart attack that she wasn't allowed to have a shower in case the shock of the water hitting her desperately thin body shocked her into an attack. She wasn't allowed to get out of bed except to transfer into a wheelchair in order to be taken to the dining room, or into the medical room to be weighed or have blood taken. They were that afraid that her life was going to end there and then she stayed in bed for six weeks.

Her body's defence system meant that she had grown hair to protect from the extreme cold felt when at such a low weight. She grew extra fine downy hair on her face, on her back and on her arms. This coupled with the pressure sores meant that she took on an almost sub-human appearance. She wasn't allowed any visitors for six weeks. One exception was on her thirty-sixth birthday when her husband and parents were allowed in. It made her so exhausted that she recognized why the visitor ban was in place. She was also allowed only one phone call a day to her husband.

I queried this with Rachael. Surely she wasn't in prison. Why would The Priory do that? She explained that the idea was to cut off all previous routines and worries, so she could concentrate purely on eating and getting well. She was allowed no other distractions. Eating normally was her job of work.

Like me, however, she wanted to be a successful patient. She had successfully got anorexia and she wanted to use The Priory to fight her anorexia so she went to every extreme to get better. She suffered horrible cramps following meals whilst her digestive system got used to food again. She had to eat six times a day. Three meals and three snacks and she always felt full to bursting but she knew that she had to eat more. She went for weeks without a bowel movement (sorry if you are having your tea at the moment). Because the bathroom door in her room, the en-suite bathroom, was locked she had to ask permission to go to the toilet. She also had to have someone watching her.

Can you imagine that depravation? The humiliation of that? I know I can't. I get embarrassed even if there is just a large gap underneath the door in public toilets when I need to go to the toilet. But someone sitting there watching you? Watching your facial movements, and the sound?

Don't even go there, but that was Rachael's life. That's what anorexia did to her. All of the bedrooms in The Priory have en suite bathrooms, but Rachael's bathroom was locked and she had to ask permission to use the toilet. So that they could monitor, frankly, what went in and what came out and there was no chance of Rachael making herself sick.

Not that she was likely to do that anyway. There was nothing going on in the toilet that The Priory didn't know about. Even in the middle of the night she would have to ring the office from her bedside phone and ask for permission to use the toilet, and a member of the staff would come along and open the toilet for her to use — and then watch her.

It has been explained to me since that once your body weight falls below 75% of the norm you cannot think properly. You don't have the resources to make cognitive thought necessarily rational. For example, your mind will constantly tell you that you are fat and should not eat, but the reality is that you are not fat. So that is why you need someone constantly monitoring you and telling you what to do. Without it, death is a distinct possibility. For the avoidance of any doubt, anorexia is the mental illness that has the highest mortality rate.

Unless you are reading this thinking, 'I know that. It is obvious that you need to eat to survive,' don't forget you are not in control. People with anorexia have a voice inside them that sits down with them at every meal and tells them they need to lose weight.

In Rachael's case, she felt that she just wanted to fade away; if there was less of her then she believed she would cause other people fewer problems. Rachael's concern was that she was the problem in other people's lives, and it was her concern for other people rather than herself that fuelled this killer illness. Rachael's wish to fade away was very, very nearly achieved.

Every week anorexic patients are weighed publicly and as you can imagine this is a huge trauma for everybody concerned. Rachael had to walk onto the scales backwards in case she caught sight of her weight flashing up on the scales.

The anorexic minx or the anorexic voices inside patients' heads sometimes tell them to drink a lot of water before being weighed. Or to somehow put weights into their underwear, but The Priory is ahead of them on that. There is no hiding place. After six weeks of this very strict regime Rachael had gained enough weight to the point where her life was considered not to be in danger and it was judged that her cognitive capacity would benefit from the therapy sessions. Her wheelchair took her to the therapy class and the comfortable lounge that we had just left.

Over some refreshed cups of coffee we spoke about her fight with the anorexic minx and the fact that she had also had treatment for harming herself.

I haven't mentioned much about harming myself. You know from earlier chapters that I tore my toenails off and inflicted wounds to the soles of my feet. I haven't said much about it because frankly, I find it disgusting. I don't understand why I do it but I know it is revolting and distressing for those around me and ultimately pointless. But if life without any toenails is easy to conceal, Rachael's self harming was much more visible.

She had cut her forearms with a carving knife. The scars were still visible, even after months, and she virtually chain smoked. She had used cigarettes to burn her forearms and also burnt and mutilated her breasts.

Still fancy anorexia? Don't bother.

The horror of her story is as terrifying as anything that a skilled fiction writer could conjure up. In total she spent more than seven months in the Priory as a patient. Anorexia got hold of her, gripped her completely and very, very nearly took her life. We would all like to be slim, but don't choose anorexia as a lifestyle. It isn't. It is death.

Since writing this I've caught up with Rachael again and after a much more enjoyable meeting Rachael told me that she and her husband have moved to Windsor and bought another house which needs a lot of work done to it, and she has been very busy renovating that house. She is a healthy size 12 again and she still has problems with food but she has recently returned from a very enjoyable river boat trip in France and she is able to go out occasionally for meals with her husband.

Rachael is no longer seeing a psychotherapist but did have treatment for two years after her discharge. She pointed out that anorexia is a sign that things in your life have gone badly wrong somewhere and that in order to recover you need to work hard at finding out what these things are and come to terms with them. Re-feeding in the Priory was just the beginning of a very long and painful process. Rachael is also extremely grateful, to say the least, to her husband, Pete, who she describes as her lifeline. Without his help this story could have had a very different and tragic ending.

CHAPTER TWELVE
When Therapy Goes Right

AS I settled into The Priory things began to change and I started to learn more about my treatment. I had been hearing people saying they had to dash off for their one-to-one meetings and I didn't really know what that meant. Soon, though, after a meeting with my consultant they advised me that I would be seeing a psychotherapist on a one-to-one basis for ongoing therapy.

That is just what you want to hear, isn't it? That you are going to be meeting a psychoanalyst. I really thought it was one of those L.A. type moments. I was dashing off to see my one-to-one therapist with my analyst.

'Talking to my analyst the other day,' I would be able to say. Or 'I don't do that because my analyst reckons I shouldn't.' But as usual I had got things totally wrong.

I began to feel much more, I suppose, comfortable about the way I was being treated. I was beginning to acknowledge that I had long running issues with food, and depression that needed to be dealt with and I was almost looking forward to meeting my new analyst.

The day came and the meeting was at one o'clock. One o'clock meant that I could skip lunch and that normally pleased me. But The Priory had got wise to that. As lunchtime approached one of the helpers on the ward came up to me and said, 'Are you going to lunch, Paul?' By now I was starting to realise that what they were really saying was, 'You are going to lunch, Paul.'

As usual I managed to think up a feeble excuse. 'Well,' I said, 'I have got my one-to-one and I really need to think about that and prepare myself.'

'Would you like something in your room instead? We can arrange that.'

At that moment Tina appeared in the doorway to my room — which I had begun to call my cell. She said, 'Come on, I am going to lunch. Come with me. I need to talk to you.'

Any meal in The Priory dining room or even in your room is an unusual experience. What you have is the dining room that on the face of it looks like the dining room of any Country House Hotel; until you notice that for every one person eating there is normally one person not eating. They are either watching the person eat, if they are from the anorexic ward, making sure they do not hide food, hide it under the table, give their food to someone else, give their food away to anyone rather than eat it. Then you have people like me who would try to eat as little as possible because of their size and I found I had an additional problem: talking to people while I was eating was very, very difficult. But at least I was going and Tina didn't really need to speak to me, but knew I would try to skip lunch.

So I had the salad with some ham and my usual yoghurt to finish off with. I felt quite pleased with myself and as one o'clock approached I made my way across to the day hospital.

The day hospital! Really the day hospital is what was the old stable block that has now been turned into consulting rooms, again rather cleverly, by those R.A.F. builders.

The original stable block has been extended substantially to cover a number of consulting rooms, maybe six or seven plus a fair-sized room that is used as a gym. Karen at reception was expecting me and was very bright and cheerful.

'Hi Paul. You here for your one-to-one?'

'Yes, that's right.'

'Just wait in the waiting room (where else?) and she'll come and get you.'

I waited for a while, flicked through all the newspapers to see if I could steal any for the ward. The waiting room is like any other waiting room in any other institution, hospital doctors' waiting room, dentist waiting room even railway waiting room. Nobody acknowledges anybody else at all. But maybe because I had become more familiar with my surroundings, maybe it was the start of getting better but I felt quite easy with the situation. People came in, I looked up and said hello. I didn't often get a reply but at least I was making the effort, I thought.

Gradually people began to disappear as their names were called and I was conscious that it was well past one o'clock now and I was still sitting there. But what the hell? I didn't have anything else to do. The old worries about not being at work started to creep back into my thoughts but there was nothing I could do. I was here and I was going to my one-to-one, like everybody else on the ward.

So, as twenty-five-past-one approached and I was beginning to think that I had been forgotten about, a lady appeared in the doorway and almost whispered my name. I leapt to my feet.

'Yes, that's me,' I said holding out my hand. 'I'm Paul.'

'Hi, I'm Karen' (name changed). She was a slight lady, and how can I put this diplomatically? — I was beginning to think I could be diplomatic again — she was a bit unkempt. Not a very nice thing to say I know but no make-up, hair just brushed off her face. She was wearing jeans and a loose cardigan.

We made our way to one of the rooms that I had passed on my way to the gymnasium occasionally and went in. It was like any other small meeting room, just two chairs set at right angles to each other, a strategically placed box of tissues, and not much else. We sat down and Karen seemed to be preoccupied, and looked through my notes in front of her. A quite meaty file that had disappeared from my room on the first evening and I hadn't seen it since. But there it was in front of her. With all the same notes — *Paul Fox, possible anorexic, bulimic, possible alcohol dependent, possible self-harm.* Even though I had only been in The Priory a few days, that first evening seemed like a lifetime ago.

Karen seemed not to want to start. I wasn't really expecting anything dramatic to happen apart from a chat. Then she reached in her bag. A sort of office-type looking briefcase, a satchel sort of thing, and pulled out a small cassette recorder. She placed it in front of us and plugged it into the mains, and switched it on so a red light was glowing in front of me.

'I'm recording our sessions,' she said rather abruptly. 'Er, I'm not confident that I'm able to help you and so I'm recording them to play to my superior.'

This took me rather by surprise. Firstly somebody admitting that they didn't really know if they could help me or not and secondly I wasn't really comfortable with the sessions being recorded. I was aware that, possibly because of the drugs, or perhaps because of my condition and even looking back albeit through a mental illness, I was rambling, and talking nonsense a lot of the time. Perhaps being over-emotional. Certainly I wasn't the Paul that most people knew at that stage. I'm not sure I even knew who I was.

Even now thinking about those tapes we made on those few occasions that I saw that lady and even after a reassurance from the Priory that the tapes had been destroyed, I still worry about them. The things I said, the things I didn't mean, how weird I sounded. Perhaps it is a measure of my illness that I didn't worry too much at the time but just felt a general uneasiness about being recorded and in such a way that was so blatant. The recorder in front of me, glowing red hot as if this was going to be a testament of my life forever.

As with everything there is a sort of health and safety talk. 'How are you feeling now? Are you suicidal? Are you harming yourself?' It is all dealt with in a very matter of fact way and, no, I wasn't feeling suicidal. I just felt very large, very uncomfortable, and used to my environment but still far from well.

I can't remember much about what we spoke about but I do recall talking a lot and Karen looking rather, not uncomfortable but, almost in pain. It wasn't me that needed the tissues or the glass of water. It was her. Soon the session came to an end. I didn't feel we had really achieved anything. I wasn't sure what we were supposed to achieve. I knew it wasn't much.

As I came out of the one-to-one with Karen I walked back across the courtyard to my cell. As I was heading towards sofa land, a lady passed me. I had seen her walking about but I wasn't sure who she was. I just assumed that she was one of the doctors.

'Hello,' she said.

'Hello.' I tried to muster up some enthusiasm.

'I think you are coming to my CBT course, aren't you?' CBT? What was that?

Suddenly, trying to shake myself out of a stupor I said, 'I'm not sure. I've just has a one-to-one.'

'Yes,' she said. She was Gillian, someone who was going to have a remarkable effect on my well-being, much more than I could even imagine at that stage. 'You've just had your one-to-one with Karen.'

'Yes,' I said.

'How did you get on?'

'O.K.,' I lied.

Over the next few days I had several more one-to-one meetings with Karen. We were getting nowhere. Even I could see that. I was the patient. I knew nothing about what she was trying to achieve. Only that we were going round in circles. The issues were my weight, not being able to fit into my clothes, not being able to eat in front of people. The only area that we seemed to move on from was alcohol. I had stopped drinking and I didn't miss it. In fact I didn't want any more alcohol and I had got to this stage on my own.

Then one meeting was cancelled. Karen wasn't well. I wasn't surprised; she never looked very well at all. Then as I went for the following one-to-one session, waiting in the waiting room as usual and trying to steal papers for sofa land, the lady I had met earlier came in.

Gillian said, 'I'm afraid that Karen has decided that she is not going to continue working here. It was on a trial basis anyway and she has decided that her health won't allow her to continue.'

I felt quite guilty at that stage. Any normal person, i.e. not me, would have recognized that this lady wasn't well. I don't know what the problem was and I do remember asking her one day as we finished the session unsatisfactorily, 'I hope you don't mind me asking, but are you OK?' She rounded on me, 'I am perfectly OK,' she said. 'I am not here for psychotherapy, unlike you.'

I was really staggered. I was just enquiring after her health. I hadn't lost all my manners and I was genuinely concerned about her appearance, which seemed to be getting worse every time I saw her. I never forgot that moment.

I am sure she meant me no harm and in fact she was trying to help me. Maybe I had come across a bit unsympathetic but I never saw her again and only ever wondered what happened to her. I hope she alright now and I hope to God that she has destroyed those tapes.

I had wild imaginings of her getting her friends round, putting a tape on her hi fi system and saying, 'Listen to this guy. He is a real fruit cake.'

I am sure now that it wouldn't happen. I just hoped that being taped was unusual. I have since learnt that it is.

Gillian sat down next to me in the waiting room and explained that she would be taking on my case. I felt immediately relieved. She seemed very easy to talk to; she knew about my case; she knew why I was there and we got on well. She was somebody I liked.

We made our way across to what I thought was just another set of offices, but again there seemed to be more consulting rooms and rooms for therapy tucked away all over the grounds of The Priory. After a rather complicated arrangement for getting in, Gillian showed me into what was obviously her office. There was a desk in one corner. I was quite pleased to see that Gillian had the same system for filing papers as I did, i.e. on the floor! Glasses were casually left on the desk together with a coffee mug. It seemed more normal than the environment that Karen had taken me to. There was of course the customary box of tissues.

We sat down and if I were looking for a time when I really did start to turn a corner that was it. Gillian said 'Look, I have read through your file. It is quite clear to me that you have a distorted view of what you look like. You have a long running eating disorder which has very nearly tripped into full blown anorexia and you have had long standing problems with depression. Throughout that you have still been able to maintain a highly pressured job, which has fuelled your anxieties; and here you are aged 43 (and a half) and I believe that you can get better. I believe you will get better but you have got to be realistic. Why don't we try and aim for the ceiling? Forget about the stars for the moment. Let us get you back to where you can objectively look at your life and change the things you need to in order to become happy.'

That was it. Through all the therapy session, joint sessions, and group sessions I had done, including the sessions where I had met Rachael and we had spoken privately about our attitude to food, I had assumed that I had to either get completely better or stay as I was. Really, I had always had a poor attitude to food. I had also slept very badly during most of my adult life. I had a way of being able to concentrate one hundred percent on something I wanted. Something I wanted to achieve, something I wanted to get and I always got there but, of course, now Gillian was able to show me, and more importantly for me to identify for myself, that those achievements had come at a terrible personal cost. Not only to me but to my family and anyone that was close to me. Concentrating very, very hard on something you want to achieve is a gift but it also a curse. That curse was about to be lifted.

CHAPTER THIRTEEN
When Therapy Goes Wrong

AS I mentioned previously it seems to me that The Priory very much encourages group therapy and I can certainly understand why.

If you are well enough to actually listen to other people talking about their problems, firstly for once you are concentrating on someone other than yourself and on their suffering. Secondly and perhaps most importantly, you can see a pattern. Everyone is there for more or less the same reasons. That is the art of getting group therapy right. Not everyone does participate, but I now understand that those who remain silent can gain just as much from the session as those of us that like to talk.

The sessions can be shared with inmates or in-patients, whatever you want to call them, and people that attend The Priory on an out-patient basis. At first I did find this unusual and there was a definite distinction between those of us that were 'banged up' and those participants who arrived in their suits and work clothes and treated it as though it was another meeting.

At first I resented that. These people couldn't be ill. What were they doing in this class? What were they doing here taking up time? They were obviously still working. But like most things, I had got it wrong. People that attended on an out-patient basis were the ones that had got it right. They were the ones who had gone to their doctor and said, 'I have got a problem with anxiety, alcohol, leaving my house.' They had been referred to a psychiatrist and had the strength and the foresight to realise that something was wrong and it needed to be corrected. They didn't wait for the almighty collapse that I had.

Gillian also took these mixed CBT classes. CBT, by the way, stands for Cognitive Behavioural Therapy. You can understand why it is shortened to CBT, can't you?

Gillian was able to split people into groups, and get the most out of them. I found that after her group sessions I was totally exhausted, but also elated. However, Gillian didn't take all of them and one day something went spectacularly wrong.

This wasn't a mixed session, with in-patients and out-patients. This was just in-patients. We went along to the normal comfortable group therapy room, just adjacent to the main lounge where Lavinia played the piano so wonderfully most evenings. First of all there were not many people there — possibly six or seven. Normally the room was packed. That was why you had to get there early to get a decent chair, one that made you look thinner.

The session was due to start at 10.30 a.m. The allotted time came and went, still no therapist. 10.45 came and went.

In the end I couldn't wait any longer. I went back to the ward and told them what had happened. They said they would get on to it. They were sure it wasn't a mistake; someone just hadn't turned up. 10.55 now and people were beginning to drift off. There were only five of us left. I was beginning to think I might as well head-off myself when suddenly the door opened rather abruptly.

I would like to tell you who it was. I really would. I believe in naming and shaming, but I don't know who it was. He didn't give us his name. The main door swung open and in walked a very well-dressed man. Probably about the same age as me, maybe slightly older, expensive shoes, tie, glasses. I would like to think not unlike my own wardrobe. He sat down in the designated leader's seat, flung his jacket round the back of the chair and said, 'Right, well, there has obviously been a cock-up.' Those were his first words and I think set the tone of the whole session.

'Is this all there is?' he said glancing around.

Muggings answered. 'Yeah, well, some people drifted off. They couldn't wait any longer.'

'They should have waited.' He snapped back at me as if it was my fault. 'OK, we are very late so let's begin. What I want you to do is all close your eyes.' We did. 'And concentrate on the reason that you are here.'

I opened one eye. So did everyone else. 'Why I am here?' I said.

'Yes, close your eyes and think about the absolute worst thing that you can think of.'

'This is a novel approach,' I thought. So I did. I concentrated on my worthless self. The fact that I was the size of a barrage balloon. The silence in the room became deafening. When I opened my eyes, everybody else's eyes were already open. A lady in the corner, that I hadn't seen before said, 'I am not sure I can do this. That is what I am trying to forget.'

'Oh, OK, then. Best forget that then. We will concentrate on something else. 'What I want you to do is split into groups.'

Muggings again, 'What? Five groups? How are we going to do that?'

Nobody moved. I was then suddenly aware that not only did I not know this guy leading the group, I didn't really know anyone else either. There was an older chap who had only been admitted the day before; he seemed quite pleasant, white haired, very well mannered. Another lady I hadn't seen before, I didn't recognise her from the ward. She had already spoken and was looking increasingly uncomfortable. Then in the corner, there was a middle-aged lady, looking decidedly uneasy. She hadn't said one word; she hadn't even raised an eyebrow at this guy's behaviour. Then I remembered that it was the first time she had ever sat in on a session. 'Not very good timing,' I thought.

'OK, then. Let's just think about our situation.'

'Are we still splitting into groups?' I said.

'No, no forget that.'

'OK,' I said. 'Lets just all think about that'

'What, the groups'?

'No, our situation.'

'Oh, OK. Everyone else's situation or my situation?'

People began to laugh. That's not what is expected and I was given a withering look. Then without warning, he seemed to go into a trance. He put his hands together as if praying and his forefingers to the end of his nose, as if he were shooting a gun up it. He just starred at the wall. Silence. It is annoying, isn't it? The silence went on and on. People began to shuffle their feet, and look nervous. After a while, a long while, I said, 'Somebody nudge him. He may be having an epileptic fit.' Again I was rounded on. It is all part of the therapy process.

I didn't realise it was part of the therapy process. I thought that we were there to talk and listen and help one another. Maybe I had got that wrong. The whole session didn't work. Those that normally spoke, like me, spoke but didn't make much sense. Those that I hadn't met, I don't know how they normally reacted in these sessions. I was just aware though that the lady who sat in the corner looked more and more as if she wished she had stayed at home. This wasn't working at all.

Now in fairness I am not a doctor. I don't know how these sessions are supposed to work. I was just a patient but I was aware that something was ticking in this lady's mind. You could almost see the cogs of her mind turning as she struggled with whether to say something or not. Again a sort of deathly silence fell over the group and I wondered what was going to happen.

For no real reason most eyes settled on this lady. Again you could see the beginnings of a thought process. Suddenly she spoke 'I.... I.....I've been so down,' she said. Not much of a comment, you might think, but it took her a great deal of courage to say those words. You could see it etched on her face. I got the impression it was the first time that she had probably ever admitted to herself or certainly spoken to anyone, least of all a few strangers, about how she felt.

After a few seconds we glanced back at our well-dressed leader. I was expecting him to say something that would encourage the lady to say more about her situation. Another long withering silence. Then without any comment at all on what the lady had said, he looked at his watch and said, 'That is the end of the session today and I'll probably see you soon.' He grabbed his jacked off the back of his chair and almost ran out of the room.

We couldn't believe it. If the therapy session itself had been a waste of time what happened afterwards was much more relevant. We all began to talk to the lady in the corner about how she felt. Unfortunately I cannot comment on her clinical state of mind because, as I say, I don't know anything about it. All I can say is that after hearing her story of a lifetime of depression I felt that she had moved on as she told us how she felt. She told us what it was like to wake up every morning wishing that you were dead. So it would seem that even when therapy goes wrong it can go right.

Let's face it. We all make mistakes. We all have bad hair days and this was just one for that particular therapist, I am sure. But it did achieve something. I now had something to contrast my sessions with Gillian against. I didn't feel as though I got anything out of that meeting myself but I felt I had helped someone else and that made it all the more special.

CHAPTER FOURTEEN
Brain Scan

I DON'T know why I have left it until now to tell you about my head injury.

It would seem, if this were a court case, to be a material fact. It was really the start of my life going very badly wrong. From the incident itself there is not very much to tell. I was drunk, coming home on the train when someone took a shine to my mobile phone. You remember the one that looks like a remote control? I had been used to getting comments from people about it. But this guy didn't want to comment on it. He wanted it. What happened next is a blur.

All I remember is a guy in a blue anorak, smelling of unwashed hair, and a short exchange that went something like, 'I'll have that.' 'Oh, no, you won't.' And yet again, like so many incidents in my life where any normal person would have let him have the phone — after all it was only a piece of plastic — I'm almost pleased with the splendid right hook I managed to land on the guy's face. In fact more than a year later my right hand still bears the scars.

So round one to me then. But round two didn't quite go as planned and he managed to hit me with something immensely heavier than his fist. I don't even remember the lights going out. All I recollect is opening my eyes and seeing the ground. The concrete next to my face was dark and there was something warm but rather sticky rolling down my head. I couldn't see properly and then I realised I couldn't open my right eye; in any case, my glasses had come off.

There was a guy standing over me; for any further editions of *Crimewatch* that might want to use this, I don't know if it was the same guy. (Helpful, eh!) Then it all goes a bit blurry. I remember a British Rail employee running up the platform saying, 'What's happened? What's happened?' and picking me up. Paramedics arrived, quickly followed by Catherine and even through the bloody haze and two astigmatisms, that were now uncorrected, I could make out that Catherine was as calm and poised as ever. Calm and poised aren't ever attributes that you would apply to me, especially when drunk, after a close encounter with the ground, and sporting an open wound to the head.

Then it was hospital. I was very confused there. I don't know now looking back whether I was having some sort of flashback. For the record, if you treated me on that night, I am sorry. The confusion is normal. The rest of it was the result of the incident.

So here I am in my second week at The Priory. I am waiting at sofa land for someone to pick me up and take me for a brain scan. I had already told Lester that I was going for a brain scan and he had rather helpfully remarked that I would probably have to take my trousers off for them to scan my brain! But the last words were if they find anything let him know. I am not sure to this day if he meant if they find a brain or if they find anything serious let him know. But I took it as concern.

I didn't have to wait long for Caroline to appear at sofa land. I thought that she was probably 17 or 18. It was like going for a trip out with my daughter. Although on this occasion she was very much in charge. I later found out that she was in her late twenties and had two children of her own. Whatever she was taking, I want some!

We got a taxi to the local hospital at Broomfield. I sat in the back. I was still feeling pretty rough at this time, so I instinctively headed for the back seat.

During the last few weeks at work I had been lucky enough to be chauffeured about, so I instinctively sat in the back. It wasn't until later that I found out Catherine would instruct drivers to sit me in the back to stop me from, as she put it, 'fiddling'. Because I couldn't sit still I had to alter the radio station, try the CD player, fiddle with air vents, switch on the air conditioning, and switch it off again. Catherine doesn't often swear but on these occasions she would normally seethe silently for a while and then shout, 'Will you fucking stop fiddling?'

So not for the first time I was in the back seat of a car on the way to hospital. But on this occasion it was not a limo; it was a minicab. Caroline engaged in polite conversation with the driver and I stared out of the window. It was only a short ride and as I got out of the car I instinctively said to the driver 'Thanks very much.' 'That's all right mate, you take care. Oh, hang on a minute,' and reaching into a door bin he pulled out a bright red and yellow pen, one of the throw away types. 'There you go, mate. Cheer up. It might never happen.' I didn't point out to him that in fact it had already happened. But I was grateful for the pen and the ride.

The inside of the hospital was suddenly an environment I wasn't used to. The interior of The Priory was so calm. No one rushed. It was sympathetically lit. The first thing that struck me was that the hospital was very bright. Secondly it was extremely noisy. It was so noisy it hurt and so bright that I was squinting. Even now, through my corrected astigmatisms, I couldn't really see where I was going.

When the door opened, I was going to see enough to wish I hadn't arrived and I wasn't there. For in front of me was a member of hospital staff who I used to work with. Margaret was a colleague's secretary who would often help me out and cover my work when my own secretary was away. She had decided to have a career change and was a senior receptionist at the MRI Unit. I was hoping she wouldn't recognise me but she did.

'Paul,' she said. 'What on earth has happened to you?' And close to tears it all came tumbling out. Margaret was professional enough not to comment on my ramblings. Instead she assured me that now that I was getting help, I would soon be back to my old self. The only problem was that my old self wasn't much good, so being reassured I would soon be back there wasn't much fun.

Another nurse approached me and asked some questions. I struggled with each one. My date of birth, my middle name, and my weight, which I wasn't sure of but I informed her it was somewhere over 20 stone. 'Are you sure?' I was positive. In fact I was still questioning whether in fact I would be able to fit into the hole in the machine that was going to scan me.

If you are not familiar with these machines, just imagine a doughnut the size of your living room and a railway track entering the hole with a stretcher on it. They get you to lie on the stretcher and then push you into the centre of the machine. It is nothing at all to worry about, but for myself I was petrified. But I was petrified then most of the time anyway.

My time came quickly. Soon I was being helped onto the stretcher and there seemed to be a lot of people around me reassuring me and telling me I would be alright. I was laid on my back and my head was placed in a sort of Tupperware box; that's the only way I can describe it. Then various ... electrodes, I suppose, were attached to my head. They tried to attach them to my head, but my hair is also overweight and has the consistency of a Brillo pad. Soon some gel was found to help control my unruly hair.

The nurse told me that I could have the option of listening to some music. You know how I feel about music so that was good for me.

'What sort of music would I like?'

'Elton John,' I replied.

'Don't think we have got any Elton John but we do have some Eagles.'

That would do. To the strains of *Hotel California* my world went black. Two pads were placed over my eyes and the Tupperware box was closed around my head. The trolley powered up and started to inch me into the centre of the doughnut. I was told to keep my hands still and for once — maybe I was getting better — I followed their advice. I crossed my hands over my chest Tutankhamen style. I am not sure how close the side of the machine was but I was aware that it was very close.

Hotel California was interrupted and through my headphones I heard the nurse who had spoken to me outside. It was a bit like listening to Jonathan Ross or Steve Wright on the radio. She was speaking but I was aware of other people conversing, too. She was obviously talking to me from the control centre. Her dulcet tones advised me to keep still and I would see lots of flashing lights.

Then I heard it. Someone in the background saying, 'What's that?' Silence. Even more silence. Even though it was only a second or two, I knew I wouldn't be hearing *Hotel California* much more.

Another voice boomed, 'What on earth it that?' The nurse replied, 'Just keep calm, Paul.' Keep calm. They had already decided I was dead.

What in God's name had they seen? To cap it all, I heard someone say, 'We have got to get him out of there!' 'Jesus,' I thought. Fear struck me. I was completely alone. I couldn't move and I was about to be given some news that I definitely didn't want to know. I strained my ears for any sound at all. All I could hear was the static electricity in my headphones. About 30 seconds later the nurse said once again, 'Paul, we are going to bring you out.'

Bear in mind that I couldn't see anything. All I could rely on was my sense of fear. I came out of that doughnut like a bullet. Whether some ejector button had been pressed, I don't know. But as soon as I was outside I tried to reach up to pull my headphones off and I was aware of people rushing towards me. It seemed like lots of people. Off came the Tupperware box. Off came the goggles.

I was surrounded by people in white coats looking rather anxious. Off came the headphones. I wanted to say, 'What is the matter? What is going on?' Then without a word they started running their fingers through my hair. Here am I about to die and they are worried about their electrodes. Then a doctor grabbed something from my hair.

'Here is it!'

'What is it? What am I dying from?'

'It is a' – he was showing me — 'it's a ladybird!'

'What?'

'It's a ladybird in your hair!'

A fucking ladybird! All this fuss over a fucking ladybird. It's never happened before. Everyone was laughing. Everyone except me. I was still petrified. Somehow a ladybird had managed to get into the machine either on my clothes or on my hair. I was soon breathing again and beginning to contemplate that maybe I wouldn't die.

As *Hotel California* came back on I was back into the machine. After a few flashing lights, it was all over and I was back in the cab on my way to The Priory.

Nothing was found — only one rather startled ladybird.

So I was OK even though I couldn't seem to keep upright or walk in a straight line.

And much to Lester's disappointment my trousers stayed in place.

FINAL CHAPTER
On My Way Home

JUST as I began to settle in to my new life at The Priory I began fortunately to get better. The combination of drugs and therapy were working. I began to feel brighter; I started to engage in conversation with people in the dining room. I didn't need Tina to go with me every time anymore. It was me asking Tina if she was ready for lunch. I was able to find my newspapers every day. I was able to locate my favourite spot in sofa land and I was even beginning to watch television and read again.

Not surprisingly, it was deemed that it was time for me to go home. I made my way round various people's rooms and said goodbye to them, wishing them well. Rachael had gone by this time and slowly I began to think about what would happen when I returned home and to work.

I was determined to get back to the office and felt I should make the leap from being unwell to working as soon as I could. I was convinced that I was going to do that. I was told by one of the nurses that I had to wait for my TTAs. TTAs. 'What on earth is that,' I thought? I just nodded as if I understood what she was talking about.

'TTAs. How long will I have to wait?' I said.

'Oh, we are just doing them now.'

So I sat down on one of the sofas in sofa land facing the office where the drugs always emerged from. Not surprisingly, it was always kept very firmly under lock and key. As I sat contemplating what TTA could stand for, I was aware that two of the young ladies from the anorexia ward were walking towards me. Between them they were dragging a very large box.

I felt as though I should get up and help but I thought it might be some sort of experiment or something like that to determine whether they were well enough to lift the box or get a box to some other part of the building. So I just looked and smiled as they came laughing along the corridor, dragging this item.

Suddenly, one of the girls said, 'Are you Paul?'

'Yes,' I said, rather surprised.

'This is for you.'

'For me? What on earth is it?'

'We don't know. We were just asked to come and find you and give it to you. It was left at reception.'

'Thanks.'

They said, 'Do you know what it is?'

'No, no I have no idea.'

But sure enough there was my name — Paul Fox, c/o Priory Hospital, Chelmsford.

The girls sat down and said, 'Do you mind if we see what it is?'

'Of course not,' I said. I started undoing the large box. The tape seemed to take ages to come off as I was still not that well coordinated. Fortunately my two delivery messengers helped me. Once the lid came off, it was clear what it was. It was a large basket of fruit in a wicker arrangement and reaching around there was a card inside. It said, 'To Paul, from all of your friends and colleagues at Layton Blackham', (my company). I was so taken aback. I never thought that they would worry about me, and having the foresight and kindness to send me such a lovely gift really did touch me.

Then my TTAs arrived! I was rather disappointed to learn that TTA stands for 'To Take Away'. So it was my supply of antidepressants that I would need for home and a letter for my doctor explaining the medication. I had already packed and Catherine had said she would pick me up from the car park, so with my wheelie suitcase and the basket of fruit balanced on top I tottered out into the car park. I didn't have to wait long and Catherine had very kindly brought my beloved red Alfa to come and pick me up.

I must admit I did feel a bit apprehensive and kept repeating that I wanted to go back to work as soon as possible but it wasn't the anorexic minx. There was another voice inside me just saying take it easy — you have learned a lot and you have come very, very close to the edge. Just take it easy. One step at a time. Gillian's advice kept surfacing in my mind. She said think about work, think about the place it has in your life and think about whether that place is the appropriate place for it to be.

I didn't quite understand that at the time but since I have got better, I do. Work for me was absolutely everything. Everything else came second to work and that was wrong. Now I had a chance to put it in its proper perspective.

Once work gets to the stage where you can think of nothing else at any time during your waking hours and all of those hours are completely taken up with thinking about it or doing it, it is the time to give it up, because no matter what you earn, or how much you say you like it, it is not worth 24/7. Ever. I only wish I had learned that earlier.

Once I got home, however, things went pretty well. I had a few problems with the antidepressants and the side effects. First of all they made my eyes sting and I became very sensitive to light. So I took to wearing my sunglasses all the time during the day and indoors. For some reason I had a strange compulsion to walk. I walked everywhere. I walked round the block, around the town, to get my hair cut and to see friends.

At the same time, whilst the choking sensation had gone from my throat, I felt as though I had a hole in it. Bizarre, I know, but I felt as though I had a hole the size of my fist in my throat. As it was approaching Christmas and starting to get cold I took to wrapping my old Air Force shawl around my neck several times. It would cover the lower part of my face as well so with the sunglasses and the shawl I looked like a trainee suicide bomber. My balance still wasn't wonderful and so I staggered from side to side.

All in all I looked a right state wandering around. You could see people ushering small children out of my way and drivers in cars reaching for the central locking buttons as I staggered by.

Lester kept up almost daily contact, but even he was beginning to remark on my appearance. 'Christ, Foxy, you don't half look a state dressed like that,' he would say in his normal diplomatic way. But he was right.

I still wasn't able to drive so relied on Catherine and friends to drive me to and fro. I remember one day going into the garage to get something and as Catherine quite rightly chose to drive her Ford Focus rather than my Alfa, the battery was soon flat. But as it was open I decided just to sit in it for a while. In the dim light of the garage the sort of half light of the interior took on a rather forlorn aspect. As I looked down I could see a piece of paper between the centre console and driver's seat. I grabbed hold of it just out of curiosity in order to throw it away.

As I looked at it I understood how out of proportion my work life had become. It was a scrap of A4 paper that I had used to write notes, normally while I was on the phone in the car. Every possible piece of space on the paper was crammed with messages saying 'phone so and so', urgent triple exclamation marks, 'urgent today', or 'very urgent'. Every message had the same tone. It was as if all of the messages were screaming at me. If you have ever done any time management courses, as I have done, you will know that if everything is urgent, then nothing is urgent.

Whatever way I folded this piece of paper it had messages on. It seems almost laughable now that these messages were the sole focus of my life at that time. As you know I love cars, but within the briefest amount of time looking round the vehicle, I recognized that I had chosen this car whilst I was unwell. Its fire-engine colour screamed urgency. Even the mismatched crushed velour upholstery did nothing to calm it down. When Lester first saw it, he got in, played with a few switches and said, 'Where's the condom machine? It will set it off nicely.'

There was just enough life in the battery for me to switch on the CD player. Music, any type of music, is another great love of mine, but all six CDs stored on the changer were all as miserable as sin! 95% of my collection was, to say the least, melancholy. Whilst I was in The Priory I remember going to music therapy. Everyone got to take one CD in, play it and then talk about it. Keen to impress, as usual, I went first. When it had finished three quarters of the class were in tears, a record apparently. The song, Elton John was the first track off the album *Blue Moves — Tonight*. Definitely music to slash your wrists to.

I decided that my Alfa was looking as sorry for itself as I was these days. I quickly went indoors. But something else had happened. I had turned another corner in my recovery. I was beginning to remember. It is bizarre and very difficult for anyone that hasn't experienced it to understand that I had huge gaps of the last few years in my memory. And my memory was something I had always prided myself on. No one can believe that I can recall my mother's 21st birthday, but I can; I was 9 months old.

I remember my father reaching into my cot to pick me up and carrying me into their bedroom and my mum opening her card. It was in the shape of a crown. My mum couldn't even remember this, but many years later on an expedition into their loft, the card was found and sure enough it was in the shape of a crown, which was what I had always maintained. Not much later than that I can envision my mother introducing me to my first hero — the very sensible Rupert Bear. I even remember that while she was reading me the story she had on her favourite perfume called Tweed. I wonder if they still make it?

It was still many months after leaving the Priory that I returned to work on one bright spring morning. I put my suit on, grabbed my briefcase and mobile phone and headed for the car. I had replaced the red Alfa with a new one, a post breakdown cool grey, with ice cool grey leather upholstery. When I got to work I felt better, calmer, able to make decisions and remember that I had made them. When I got into difficulty I thought back to Gillian, telling me to take one step at a time and that ultimately, nothing was that important.

It's true of course that ultimately, unless you are a brain surgeon or an air traffic controller the hours and minutes spent at work are not that important. Normally, nobody dies. And I want so much to tell you that everything was perfect. In many ways it was. Everybody treated me well and I had some wonderful e mails and texts from people I hardly knew wishing me well and telling me that they were glad to see me back.

It would be wonderful to end my story here with the sun shining over a smiling Paul getting back to work, with everything else in his life sorted and back in perspective. But sadly things had changed forever, people's perception of me changed from the day I walked back into the office, and although everybody treated me kindly, I could see a slight concern in their eyes and a slight hesitation in their voice.

Most of my story has been about a form of mental illness that can affect anyone and everyone, from any walk of life. I hope that I have been able to convey that we shouldn't view mental illness any differently to 'physical' illnesses like heart attacks or strokes, but we do.

My journey into and out of The Priory has been a fundamental turning point of my life and I will never forget the time that I spent in there, including the people I met - patients and professionals alike. I believe that the Priory provided a safe and protective environment for me to fully understand my illness and to work with professionals to put things right and fundamentally change the long-held deeply embedded attitudes that were so unhealthy. I came to realise that I had suffered from an eating disorder since my late teens, and had never fully acknowledged it, let alone had it treated. I was also a very driven person, which in itself was a good thing, but it went far too far and ultimately turned into an illness. I still don't fully understand the reasons why I harmed myself and this is probably the episode that I am most uncomfortable with. My relationship with alcohol is now much better and I am able to enjoy the odd glass of wine knowing that I won't be compelled to drink an entire case.

The new friends that I made during my time in the Priory still continue to enrich my life, and friends that helped me during my time there and since I have come out have been an enormous source of encouragement and support. It isn't possible to name everybody here for all sorts of reasons, but I would just like to say how much I appreciate everybody's help. For all the phonecalls, visits, texts and e mails that are just too numerous to mention. But thank you, thank you, thank you to everyone concerned, and to the Priory as an organisation.

There is nothing else to say and it is time for me to put the light out. I have been sleeping at odd times and writing this has been a help to me, but I have been feeling very, very tired lately. Oh, well, I am sure it will pass.

Printed in the United Kingdom
by Lightning Source UK Ltd.
126802UK00001B/196-198/A